THE
OLD
FRONT
LINE

The Centenary of the
Western Front in Pictures

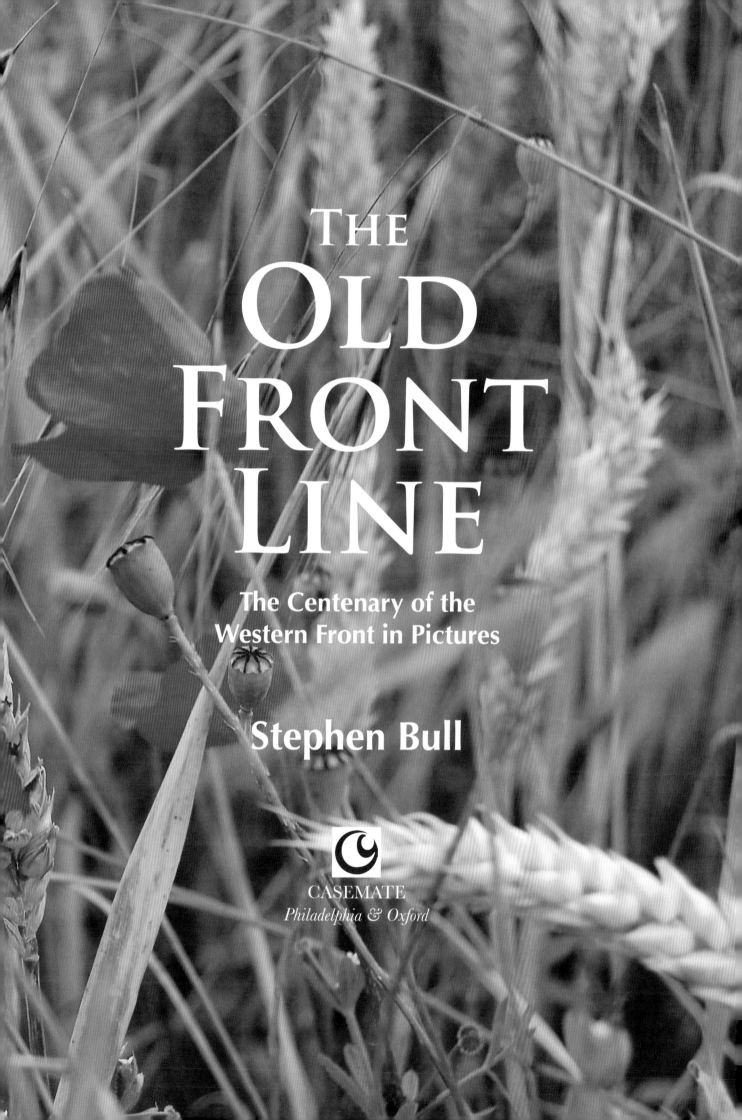

THE OLD FRONT LINE

The Centenary of the Western Front in Pictures

Stephen Bull

CASEMATE
Philadelphia & Oxford

Page 1: *Langemarck German Cemetery.*

Previous page: *Poppies and corn on the battlefield at Ovillers, Somme.*

Right: *Cabaret Rouge British Cemetery takes its name from a cafe that used to stand nearby. The cemetery was started in March 1916. there are 7,655 burials from the Great War here, nearly 4,500 of which are of unidentified soldiers.*

CONTENTS

Published in the United States of America and Great Britain in 2014 by
CASEMATE PUBLISHERS
908 Darby Road, Havertown, PA 19083
and
10 Hythe Bridge Street, Oxford, OX1 2EW

Copyright 2014 @ Stephen Bull

ISBN 978-1-61200-230-9

Cataloging-in-publication data is available from the Library of Congress
and the British Library.

10 9 8 7 6 5 4 3 2 1

Printed and bound in China

For a complete list of Casemate titles please contact:

CASEMATE PUBLISHERS (US)
Telephone (610) 853-9131, Fax (610) 853-9146
E-mail: casemate@casematepublishing.com

CASEMATE PUBLISHERS (UK)
Telephone (01865) 241249, Fax (01865) 794449
E-mail: casemate-uk@casematepublishing.co.uk

INTRODUCTION

A century on from World War I Western Europe is still gashed by a broad sinuous line snaking its way from the Channel Coast to Switzerland. This strip of the concentrated architecture of war and memorials of peace, contains the mortal remains of over three million dead soldiers. Many have no known grave, and others lie in mass graves, in what was easily the most significant killing ground of 1914–18. It is as Frederick Voigt, a British soldier of German parentage, observed, 'a stupid, terrible and uncouth monster.' Yet, just as battles pushed No Man's Land back and forth with time and there is physically more than one front line, there have also been many different interpretations of the Western Front. For some it is the ultimate monument to futility; to others a warning, or a symbol of fortitude and sacrifice. Yet, and particularly for the young, it is becoming something more hopeful, a place of mystery, wonder, and even of adventure into a past where discoveries can be made not only about war and history in general, but the very personal past of the lives of one's own ancestors.

Moreover, the meaning of the Western Front has changed radically over time. Between 1914 and 1918 the names of its villages, forts, and rivers and the heights of its hills were the essential markers by which both generals and the European public at large gauged progress, or the lack of it, towards the ultimate goal of victory and the end of what had become an increasingly exhausting struggle. Newspapers were not allowed to report on many aspects of the war for reasons of security, and rarely gave m uch more than the haziest notion of strategy. They were, however, fed the names of villages and hamlets, most already abandoned and some entirely obliterated from the landscape, as evidence of success. So it was that many civilians became as familiar with the names of the Verdun forts, or the villages of Flanders and Picardy or the Argonne, as they were with Balaklava or Waterloo. Many were unaware how insignificant those settlements really were, and even on military trench maps names like Thiepval and Passchendaele were left much more as an often forlorn

attempt to aid navigation, and warn what their cellars might now contain, than as any indication that these places still operated as living settlements. Arguably much more important figures on these wartime maps were the red and blue lines, the spots, dots, hatching and crosses that indicated trenches, machine gun nests, wire and pillboxes.

One of the first serious attempts to describe the battlefields was John Masefield's 1917 volume *The Old Front Line*. Masefield had, at first, thought to write a volume about the battle of

Dans les tranchées

Below left: *The game of war: a contemporary French postcard* Dans les tranchées *(in the trenches). Until at least late 1916 the French were indubitably the senior partner of the Entente on the Western Front. Military deaths totalling approximately 1.4 million would adversely impact French demography for decades.*

Below: *French scene 1915, showing typical elements of fire trench design. In this example the garrison man a fire step, and shoot through loopholes providing both protection and concealment. To the rear of the walkway is an additional deeper channel for drainage. The cylinders are food containers.*

the Somme, but like journalists of the time, was stymied by lack of access to official documents. He fell back on describing the terrain upon which the battle had been fought, and produced a lyrical and evocative picture in which he both looked forward to victory, and imagined how the fields of war would appear in future. He foresaw a time in which 'all this frontier of trouble' would be forgotten, the trenches filled in, the plough erasing the 'look of war'. In many ways, therefore, Masefield is our starting point, and what we are attempting here is an answer to his imaginings that enjoys not only the advantages of modern digital colour photography and access to memoirs and documents unreleased, or even unwritten, in 1917, but the very great luxury of hindsight. For Masefield's victory, expensive as it was, was indeed won, and a century on a less partisan and much more inclusive sketch can be attempted.

To an extent John Masefield was correct, for by the time of his death in 1967 much of the Western Front had not only returned to farming or nature, but been entirely damned by a new generation who saw only folly in the belligerent activities of their fathers. By now the orthodox popular view of the 'war to end all wars' was that it had been more stupid than pretty well any other, before or since. Gradually the conflict had come to be viewed through the eyes of the War Poets, perhaps more accurately 'Anti-War Poets', skilled and emotive wordsmiths such as Owen and Sassoon, masters of the description of the hopelessness and death, which were indeed one important aspect of the front. Only comparatively recently has this verdict been systematically questioned. For 'mud and blood' were only ever part of a complex story, involving diplomatic and political failure, technical and inventive ingenuity, an incredible mass mobilisation of nations and industry, and a change in attitudes to war, even as it progressed. Passage of time and increased information has given us a far more nuanced picture and one which allows a far wider variety of interpretation, both of the Western Front, and of the war itself. Arguably we have become much freer about what we can say, as the passing years make the front less of a living wound, and more a part of history. With some degree of detachment it also becomes possible to make comparisons with other great fortifications of the past—Hadrian's Wall, the Great Wall of China, or the forts and castles of antiquity.

Even before the struggle was over, the Western Front became a place of pilgrimage, with the first pioneers of the many thousands of grieving parents, wives, and siblings wanting to gain comfort from seeing the place where their son, husband, or brother had fallen, and to visit a grave. The lack of a definitive final resting place for the many torn beyond recognition or buried by bombardment would later be partially filled by memorials to the missing, such as those erected by Britain, the United States, and Canada. As the Michelin guide *Battlefields of the Marne 1914*, written even before the Armistice was signed, explained, a visit to the front, '... should be a pilgrimage, not merely a journey across ravaged land. Seeing is not enough, one must understand: a ruin is more moving when one knows what has caused it; a stretch of country which might seem dull and uninteresting to the unenlightened eye, becomes transformed at the thought of the battles which have raged there.' This idea, of the front as

Right: *Archaeologist Martin Brown at work during extensive excavations on the slopes below Messines. In addition to the usual crop of shells, this dig mapped the line of the German trenches and discovered a spade still stuck deep in the frozen mud. For several years an employee of the British Ministry of Defence, and more recently a consultant with the WYG Group, Martin has been a leading light of the long-term Plugstreet Project.*
The best Western Front archaeology has become increasingly professional in recent years, rescuing information and artefacts prior to developments, as well as informing research and tourism initiatives.

Below: *Outside the newly redeveloped In Flanders Fields Museum, Ypres, a group seeing the Western Front by bicycle, 2013. As green and health-conscious alternatives walking and cycling promise less intrusive forms of tourism, combined with an ability to reach places inaccessible to motor vehicles. Tour courtesy of Bike and Culture Flanders.*

Left: *A French demarcation stone near the Chemin des Dames. Designed by sculptor Paul Moreau Vauthier (1871–1936), these markers, about 3ft (1m) in height, were erected to show the limit of the German advance of 1918. One per kilometre (5/8 of a mile) of front was the original idea, later reduced to 240, and far fewer were actually placed between 1920 and 1927, with some added subsequently and others destroyed, mainly in World War II. A recent count lists 96 stones in France and 23 in Belgium. There are three basic types, depicting French, Belgian or British steel helmets and equipment.*

Below: *Visitors on a battlefield tour examine the 1957 memorial to the heroes and martyrs of the French offensive of 40 years earlier, located 10 miles (16km) east of Reims on the D931. Its steps mark the years of war. The struggle referred to is the Nivelle offensive, commenced on 16 April 1917. The new French Commander-in-Chief, Robert Nivelle, promised great things, deploying over a million men, 7,000 artillery pieces, and tanks between Roye and Reims, focused on the Chemin des Dames ridge. In the event the tanks were shot to pieces and the attack quickly faltered. Morale suffered a heavy blow, the rumbles of mutiny began and Nivelle was replaced by Petain within weeks.*

Introduction

Opposite: *German mass grave at the Auberive cemetery, Champagne. In this veritable cemetery complex are sections for not only Germans, but French and Poles. The number of German fallen interred here is 5,359, and of these 2,237 are laid in this overgrown mass grave.*

1914

ICH HABE EINEN
GUTEN KAMPF
GEKAEMPFT
II. TIM. 4,7

Above: *Monument to the Weimar Landsturm at Mézières-Charleville (today, Charleville-Mézières), near Sedan. The 1914 battles of the frontiers were every bit as costly as what followed and led to the rapid erection of many memorials, some of them surprisingly elaborate, and many of which were later destroyed or dismantled. This example, bearing the motto 'I have fought a good fight' and the 1914 Iron Cross, was adorned with a realistic representation of German infantry equipment.*

place of pilgrimage, gathered strength in the immediate postwar years as with the coming of peace dangers receded and transport links were restored.

Battlefield visits rapidly extended to veterans, and to their families and children, some of whom were too young to have known those whose graves they were taken to see. Comradeship and curiosity joined mourning as motives to view, or revisit, the front. There had of course been well-heeled tourists before 1914, enjoying the spas of Northern Europe, the grand tours of Italy, or the liners of the oceans. Arguably, however, what began in the interwar period on the Western Front was a new phenomenon: the first stirrings a sort of worthy and highly respectable form of mass tourism, an essentially classless journey with moral purpose. Nevertheless the memorials, battlefield parks, and neat rows of graves, most of them still much the same now as when they were erected in the 1920s, were originally intended as solace to those who survived and the families of the dead. Solemn promises of maintenance 'in perpetuity' were regarded as the minimum debt of thankful nations to those who had struggled or made the ultimate sacrifice. As Sir Frederic Kenyon, scholar and Director of the British Museum, put it in 1918,

'Those who are interested—and hundreds of thousands must be most deeply and poignantly interested—in the treatment of our dead in France and Belgium, may rest assured that no labour is spared, and nothing that careful thought can provide is wanting to pay the tribute of reverence and honour which is due to those that have fallen for their country.'

In many ways the centenary leaves the Western Front at an important historical crossroads, for now all those who fought are gone, and even their surviving children are generally of very advanced years. Where once the main threats to preservation and noble visions of memorialisation were agricultural, now housing, new roads, industry, and vandalism have all begun to encroach. A more insidious form of change is arguably the proliferation of new memorials, some out of keeping with their surroundings, others entirely anachronistic, and a few at least of which are erected more with a view to promoting modern agendas, than with the commemoration of the past. Museums and viewing points are likewise extremely valuable when handled and positioned sensitively, but there remains the danger, that, like the *Butte du Lion* at Waterloo, well-intentioned commemoration will eclipse the original, or steal it to support partisan historical judgement. Perhaps most significantly, in a world in which recession bites the living, fewer people are inclined to grace the long dead with meaningful budgets. Though this sounds like a very modern issue it is one to which some veterans, like Edmund Blunden, were alive to even in the 1960s.

Increasingly it is beginning to appear the price of long term preservation of what remains of the Western Front will be acceptance its role and use will change, little by little. Some of the brooding sadness will have to lift, and the landscape absorb the reality that learning and tourism, in their broader senses, have roles to play. Somehow indeed the originally

forbidding and bleak 'foreign fields' of war already give many citizens of various nations a sense 'of belonging', or 'identity', when other expressions fail. How far democratisation and popularisation will have to go, and how quickly, is a live debate for all the former combatant nations, and particularly for the governments of France and Belgium upon whose soil history has dumped the main weight of this responsibility.

For France both the iconic landscape of Verdun and the 1918 Armistice site at Compiègne remained important living—and internationally sensitive—memorials for many years after the war, the latter being so especially galling to the defeated that Hitler demanded the same location for French capitulation in 1940. Thereafter the railway carriage in which both documents were signed was carted away to Berlin, and the site slighted. In their turn the French later used German prisoner of war labour to restore the site, even installing a reproduction carriage after 1945. In 2014 Franco-German relations are hugely improved, and Gallic pride has arguably found much more positive expression in exceeding her neighbours in the quality and expense of her commemorations. Moving somewhat aside from the heroically stoic, and now possibly negative, image of Verdun, focus was shifted to the Marne with the start of the Museum of the Great War project at Meaux in 2005. Formal inauguration of this major facility, situated conveniently close to the French capital, was marked by President Sarkozy on 11 November 2011, and numerous visitors were flowing through by 2013. Nevertheless other sites, including Verdun, are receiving considerable makeovers, and Canada has been equally swift off the mark in France, particularly with the restoration of the memorial at Vimy.

For the Belgians in particular, as a small nation with two distinctly different cultures under one flag and a state that survived World War I only by the narrowest of margins, the centenary is a vital matter, and one that is being seized upon not only as duty, but as opportunity. In 2011 the Flemish Peace Institute, sponsored by the Flemish Government, surveyed the public and researched the matter, coming to the conclusion that a marking of the centenary should be 'war commemoration with a focus on peace', emphasise education, and 'cultural heritage' as well as architectural heritage. The Flemings also put forward aspirations for an international commitment to keep the

Opposite: *Detail of the memorial to four French corporals erected at Suippes in 2007. These men of 21st Company, Infantry Regiment 136, were shot to 'encourage the others' on 17 March 1915. After the war the widow of Cpl Theo Maupas campaigned for their exoneration, which was finally achieved in 1934.*

Left: *The uniform of French infantryman, c.1914, seen at the Musée de la Grande Guerre, Meaux. The dark blue tunic with bright red trousers and a kepi worn in the first months of war proved impractical. Within a year a new uniform of 'horizon blue' and a steel helmet were introduced.*

Below: *Just a tiny part of the vast collection of German Pickel-hauben in the collection at Fort Pompelle.*

Below right: *The shattered remains of Fort de Liouville on a hill between St Mihiel and Apremont. Built in the 1870s and heavily bombarded with its heavy armament damaged or destroyed in the autumn of 1914, it held out for the entire war.*

Below: *A rusting German 77mm field gun, wooden wheels rotted, at the small enclosed battlefield park in the shadow of the Notre Dame de Lorette cemetery. Authentic trophies add considerably to Western Front sites but long-term open-air preservation is almost impossible. Bringing such pieces undercover and replacing them with replicas or photographic panels is one way forward.*

Opposite: *The Cross of Sacrifice at Menin Road South. In this cemetery, designed by Sir Reginald Blomfield, 1,657 men are buried or commemorated. Amongst them are 78 memorials to men believed to be buried here or at Menin Road North whose graves were destroyed. The Cross of Sacrifice—also designed by Blomfield—in various sizes is a common element to British cemeteries containing more than 40 burials.*

memory of the war alive, and to have the 'remembrance landscapes' of the Somme, Marne, and Yser recognised as UNESCO world heritage sites. This internationalism would be based partly on the Western Front being viewed as a universal experience: as the report explained, 'over fifty present day states were involved in the warfare on the Western Front. Soldiers from five continents came to Flanders to fight in the trenches and often also to die and be buried there.' At an early stage decisions were made to refit the In Flanders Fields Museum at Ypres, add a new wing to the Passchendaele Memorial Museum at Zonnebeke, and to undertake extensive archaeological surveys. Both the museum projects were completed well before time and archaeology continues. Additionally, with awareness that Ypres and Tyne Cot could become overcrowded in 2014, smaller projects commenced at Nieuwpoort and Lijssenthoek, the latter receiving a new visitor centre.

Just maybe, and with healing of time, it will one day become possible to appreciate the Western Front and its history in the same way as one might love mountains or paintings, without unnecessary irreverence— but also without feeling guilty for doing so.

FORT St MIHIEL

Above *The Souain 'ant hill', Champagne, scene of bitter fighting in early 1915, when Gen Géraud Réveilhac repeatedly attacked a modest German vantage point. Unsatisfied with the performance of his troops, the general is said to have wanted his guns turned upon them, something the artillery commander refused to do without written order. In any event courts martial were ordered and four corporals were executed (see also p.14). Gen Réveilhac was relieved of command in 1916. The incident inspired the novel* Paths of Glory, *and the Stanley Kubrick film of the same title.*

Above right: *The monument in Peuvillers German military cemetery in the Eastern Argonne. Begun in an orchard at the end of August 1914 this cemetery is one of the smaller German examples, containing 967 dead from various engagements. The sculpture is based on a south German design of a mourner behind a gate, above the motto Hier Ruhen Deutsche Soldaten (Here rest German soldiers).*

Right: *German soldiers with a captured French 8mm St Étienne Mle 1907 machine gun. This model was an air-cooled, gas-operated design widely used in the early part of the war, and almost 40,000 were made before production was discontinued. The cartridges are held in 25-round metallic strips and fed into the side port by the loader.*

The unusual Russian chapel at Saint-Hilaire-le-Grand in the Champagne, built in 1937, is dedicated to the 6,100 Russian soldiers who fell in France, and stands adjacent to a cemetery and mass grave. Four Russian brigades fought in the west from 1916, and even after the revolutions of 1917 and the disbandment of the brigades some troops volunteered to stay on and fight for France.

AUX SOLDATS RUSSES

MORTS AU CHAMP D HONNEUR

EN FRANCE

1916-1918

Right: *The Liverpool Scottish in action at Bellewaarde, 1915. Much of this part of the battle-field disappeared under a 130-acre theme park in 1954.*

Below: *The wounded outnumbered the dead by about three to one. Facial injuries, such as these preserved in casts of the faces of French soldiers in the museum at Meaux, were widespread. New Zealander Sir Harold Gillies, a pioneer of facial reconstruction, observed that the problems encountered were traumatic and massive.*

Opposite, above: *Archaeological finds on display at the Memorial Museum Passchen-daele, at Zonnebeke.*

Opposite, below: *World War I weapons on display at the major new Musée de la Grande Guerre, Meaux. Described as a museum of 'history and society' the collection exceeds 50,000 items.*

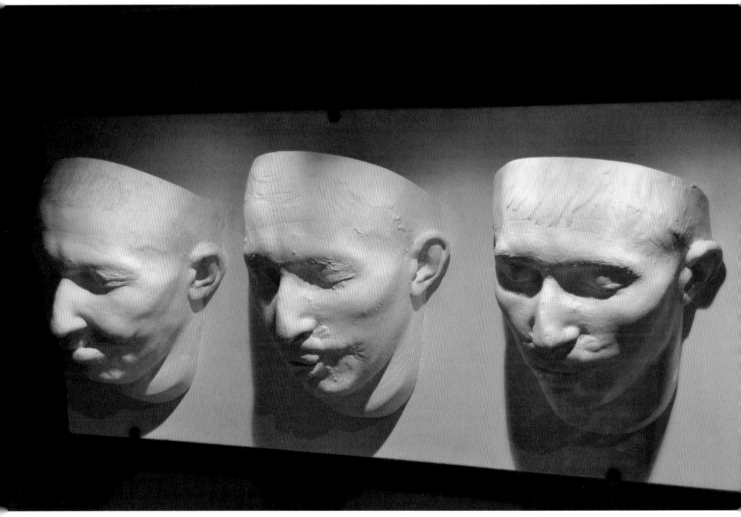

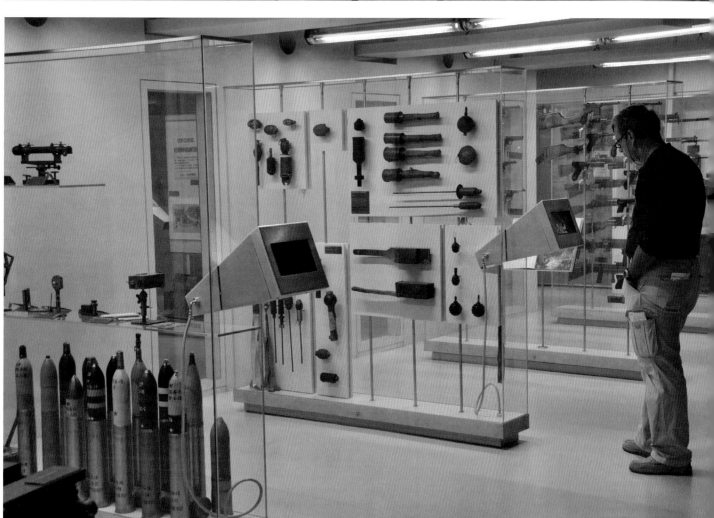

Above: *The entrance to the preserved trenches at Sanctuary Wood. Respect, history and commercialisation now exist in fragile balance. Making the Western Front relevant and interesting to new generations without losing its essential character is a real challenge of the 21st century.*

Above right: *Some imaginative new display techniques at the Centre d'interprétation Marne 14–18, Suippes, combining sound, light, film and trenchscape. Suippes lay on the old Champagne front, scene of four major battles: during the first winter of the war through to March 1915; from September 1915; during the spring of 1917; and finally in the summer of 1918. Along with other troops, French Fourth Army was heavily engaged in all four battle of the Champagne.*

Right: *The British memorial to the missing at La Ferté-sous-Jouarre on the bank of the Marne. Though predominantly a French action, British troops were also committed and it is here that the 3,740 British troops that fell in the battles of Mons, Le Cateau, the Marne and Aisne, but have no known grave, are commemorated.*

Opposite: *The Cabaret Rouge British Cemetery in winter. Named after a small red brick cafe destroyed by shellfire in March 1915, this site at Souchez north of Arras came into use as a cemetery a year later. Many of the early burials were fatalities from 47th (London) Division and the Canadian Corps, but remains from many other cemeteries were concentrated here after the war.*

Above left: *Extensive re-excavation of trenches in the Notre Dame de Lorette memorial park. Maintaining trenches in anything like their original condition requires work, not only due to the wear and tear from visitors, but because of soil movement. To repair fieldworks sensitively requires knowledge of their construction, something not always available.*

Left: *The Creute Montparnasse stone quarry on the Chemin des Dames front had been in use since in early 19th century. Captured by the Germans in 1914, and re-christened the Barbarossa Höhle, it was quickly brought into use as a massive underground shelter. Recaptured later in the war, it was also used by French troops.*

Above: *German officers at the end of a day of game shooting behind the lines. The officers carry shotguns and, centre, a dreiling triple-barrelled rifle-shotgun combination weapon. An other rank, foreground with the dog, acts as beater and porter of the game 'bag'. Sport was but part of the story: hunting added to the supply of fresh meat and relieved monotony.*

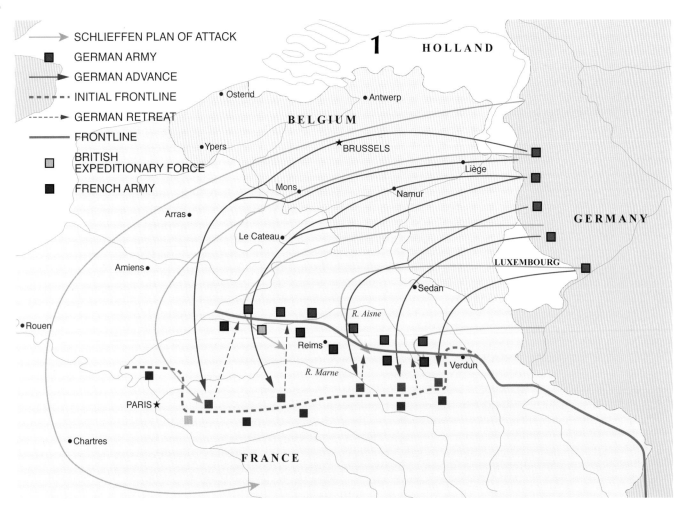

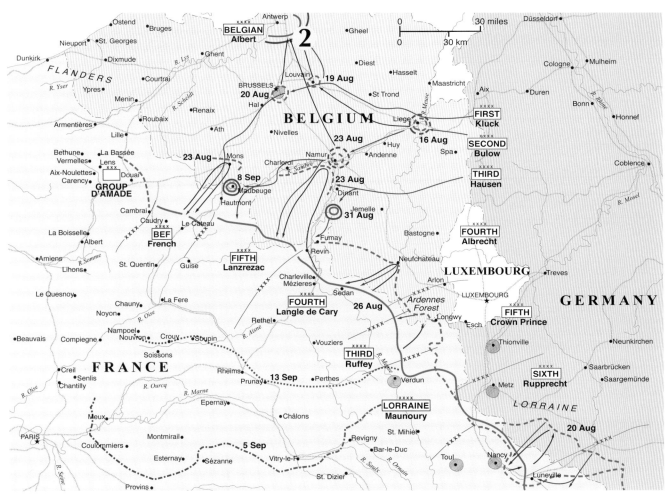

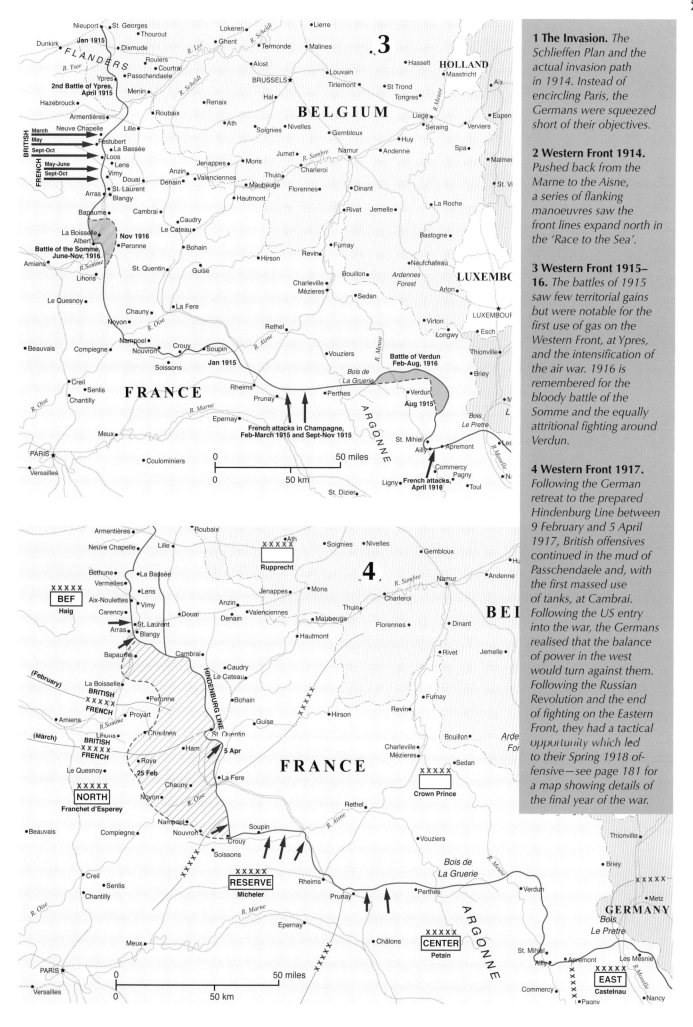

1 The Invasion. *The Schlieffen Plan and the actual invasion path in 1914. Instead of encircling Paris, the Germans were squeezed short of their objectives.*

2 Western Front 1914. *Pushed back from the Marne to the Aisne, a series of flanking manoeuvres saw the front lines expand north in the 'Race to the Sea'.*

3 Western Front 1915–16. *The battles of 1915 saw few territorial gains but were notable for the first use of gas on the Western Front, at Ypres, and the intensification of the air war. 1916 is remembered for the bloody battle of the Somme and the equally attritional fighting around Verdun.*

4 Western Front 1917. *Following the German retreat to the prepared Hindenburg Line between 9 February and 5 April 1917, British offensives continued in the mud of Passchendaele and, with the first massed use of tanks, at Cambrai. Following the US entry into the war, the Germans realised that the balance of power in the west would turn against them. Following the Russian Revolution and the end of fighting on the Eastern Front, they had a tactical opportunity which led to their Spring 1918 offensive—see page 181 for a map showing details of the final year of the war.*

Chapter 1
Brave Little Belgium

Men of 4th Battalion, East Lancashire Regiment occupy trenches at Nieuwpoort, September 1917. Note the use of a mirror as a simple periscope to observe over the trench. Following the race to the sea in 1914, the left of the Allied line lay on the Belgian coast near Nieuwpoort. With the defeat of the German attempt to break though at neighbouring Ramskapelle the front was locked solid. There are several monuments in the vicinity today including the Yser memorial, one to King Albert I and the British memorial to the missing of the Antwerp expedition.

Opposite: *The Belgian memorial in the old town of Poperinge, hop-growing centre of Flanders. In 1914 the Belgian army comprised seven field divisions plus 65,000 fortress troops, and was thus considerably larger than the original British Expeditionary Force. Belgian military deaths in 1914–1918 exceeded 58,000.*

Below right: *Louvain, with its many picturesque medieval buildings, was badly hit during 1914, and its famous library deliberately gutted by fire. Though many irreplaceable items were destroyed, after the war it was rebuilt and restocked with the assistance of the United States and UK. In Louvain burned buildings rebuilt after the war were marked with distinctive stone tablets showing the date 1914, a fiery torch and a German bayonet.*

Below: *The grave of Pte John Parr of the Middlesex Regiment at St Symphorien military cemetery just east of Mons. Pte Parr of North Finchley is believed to be the first British fatality of the war, being killed on 21 August 1914. He set off on a bicycle scouting mission, but did not return. Parr enlisted under age, being probably only 16 at the time of his death. St Symphorien, which also contains German graves, has been selected by the UK government as the scene for a commemorative event to mark the centenary of the commencement of hostilities.*

From at least the medieval era the Low Countries became an uncomfortable crossroads for armies: 'the cockpit of war' in Europe. In 1914 history would repeat itself, and not for the last time, as conflict in Western Europe thrust suddenly upon one of its smallest nations. In some ways this was unexpected, since the flashpoint of the summer of 1914 lay far to the east. Minor wars had already disturbed the Balkans, and the assassination of the Austrian Archduke Ferdinand at Sarajevo on 28 June focused attention sharply upon fraught relationships between the Austro-Hungarian Empire and Slavic neighbours. A partial mobilisation by Russia, and Kaiser Wilhelm's German 'blank cheque' of unconditional support to Austria, led many to expect the tramp of marching feet, into Serbia, and perhaps on the borders of Russian Poland. Yet a web of alliances, strategic realities, diplomatic failure, the advent of war 'by timetable' based on railways, plus inflexible planning, meant that these eventualities would be the least of international worries. Both France and Germany ordered general mobilisation on 1 August.

The invasion of neutral Belgium was triggered by German calculation that her perceived encirclement by the Entente powers, France, Russia, and Britain could only be broken by a massive and swift pre-emptive strike. Since Russia was huge and her 'steamroller' was likely to gear up slowly, Germany would therefore use the vast majority of her military force in the West, to smash France 'before the leaves had fallen'. This would prevent a two-front war, and if necessary allow Germany and her Central Powers partner, Austria-Hungary, to deal with Russia at leisure. The basic plan, originally laid down by General Alfred von Schlieffen well before the war, was bold and arguably administratively brilliant in the best traditions of the German General Staff, but carried with it flaws and assumptions that would ultimately be its undoing.

Perhaps most crucially it was based on the pessimistic notion that, war being inevitable, France and Russia could never be separated diplomatically: nor did it allow room for hope that other powers such as

RECHT   TROUW

BATTHEU, GERARD.   D'AMOUR, CYRIEL.
BEHEYT, SYLVAIN.   DANNEEL, OSCAR.
                    DEBERGH, HENRI.

Britain, the Ottoman Empire, or Italy, the latter already at least notionally a partner, might be bribed, negotiated or cajoled into more positive stance before tested by crisis. The Schlieffen plan prepared for the worst, and the worst it would produce. A socially maladroit Kaiser, his diplomats, and the expansion of the German Navy in opposition to Britain, all made the job the army would be expected to perform far more difficult. The scheme was also inflexible in that it appeared to allow for no scenario under which limited war might be fought in the East, or only by the Austro-Hungarians. Such conflicts might have painted France an aggressor, and left Britain, and ultimately the United States, little pretext for action. Technically and tactically the plan also had uncertainties. Schlieffen himself had been concerned that the big 'right hook', intended to encircle Paris, should be a strong as possible. Though the latest German Chief of Staff, Moltke the Younger, was broadly convinced of this requirement, he tinkered with detail.

Moreover, the burgeoning size of forces, improvements to weaponry, and relative lack of rail lines and good roads meant that squeezing four or more armies rapidly over the Rhine and into northern France, without crossing Dutch or Belgian borders, was never a viable proposition. In Moltke's final version of the plan Belgium would be traversed, but the Netherlands not encroached. However, it was also assumed, unrealistically, that the Belgians would either grant free passage through their territory to hundreds of thousands of German soldiers, or offer only token resistance. In a negative way the invasion of Belgium also solved a problem for Britain. By the treaty of 1839, also signed by France and Prussia, she was committed to the guarantee of Belgian independence: in honouring this treaty Britain could intervene with clear conscience and popular mandate. She could also fulfil her own historic interest in protecting the Channel coasts from domination by any one foreign power, meanwhile standing by her obligations to France and Russia. What appeared murky and conditional was now clear: the modest British Expeditionary Force under Field Marshal Sir John French would be sent to stand at the left shoulder of the French armies for the defence of Belgium. The German

Below: *A good idea of the appearance of trenches in the flooded landscape of Flanders. Here German troops have dug down a little, but have also been forced to build upward with sandbags, so creating a 'box' trench. Such constructions gave cover but were painfully obvious targets on top of the surrounding morass. Note how this front-line trench is divided into bays, so limiting the effects of blast or small-arms fire along the void.*

assumption that Britain would not intervene had been disabused on the strength of what Chancellor Bethmann-Hollweg famously described as 'a scrap of paper'.

As the German army crossed the Belgian border on 4 August, the French responded immediately, striking into Germany further south following their own ill-fated Plan XVII. The battles of the frontiers had begun, threatening to become a massive military revolving door pivoting around Luxembourg. On the German side about 1.5 million troops were in action in the West, deployed in seven armies: very soon, and taking French, Belgians and British together, the Entente commitment would not be very much less. At Liège a swift *coup de main* was foiled and the forts there besieged, super-heavy artillery being brought up for the purpose. Skirmishes near Namur subsequently coalesced into similar bombardments. The Germans pushed on resolutely across Belgium, if more slowly than expected, but the French advance south of Metz was later politely described as having 'failed tactically'. With large bodies of men attempting to attack against modern quick-firing artillery, machine guns, and magazine rifles losses swiftly mounted.

With the Belgian army buying time the BEF managed to cross the Channel, gathering in the region of Maubeuge by 20 August, the day Brussels fell to General von Kluck's First Army. The British first clashed with the enemy when cavalry patrols met east of Mons two days later, and it was around Mons they stood and fought their first major action on 23 August. As the British official history remarked, the infantry fought with a 'characteristic obstinacy'. The Germans advanced into the face of rapid rifle fire and machine guns, suffering from what a German staff report later called 'bloody losses'. Nevertheless the much weaker BEF was in danger of being surrounded and overwhelmed. Accordingly Sir John French ordered the retreat. In the words of the German official account, 'A decision had seemingly not been obtained. Only the envelopment of the British by the right wing of the Armies could lead to this.' To avoid such an eventuality the BEF began the exhausting and perilous retreat from Mons. Three days later the British stood at Le Cateau, before again being pushed from the field and escaping before they could be encircled.

German Landsturm *infantry. Swift and massive expansion of the German army was made possible both by conscription and a series of reserve formations that even in peacetime continued a citizen's military obligations until his 45th year. After compulsory service in the standing army a soldier was placed in the reserve proper; he then passed to the* Landwehr, *and finally to the* Landsturm. *In time of emergency all these types of troops could be embodied simultaneously.*

Opposite, above: *The 'lonely grave' of a German Guard dragoon at Fort Loucin near Liège, 1914. The forts were pounded into submission and Loucin, west of the city, was one of the last to fall, and it was from here that a wounded Gen Gérard Leman, the Belgian commander, was carried out on 15 August.*

Opposite, below: *The town square of Mons at night. A century earlier, 4th Battalion, Royal Fusiliers, rested here just before the British Army fought its first major engagement of the war. Sir John French had agreed to hold the Mons Conde canal line, so protecting the left of Gen Charles Lanrezac's Fifth Army. On the morning of 23 August Alexander von Kluck attacked. Despite inflicting heavy losses the British were in danger of being overwhelmed, and so retreated the following evening.*

Below: *Parisian Renault taxi at the Meaux museum. Manufactured prior to World War I, the Renault had an 8hp engine. Famously 600 were requisitioned by the French Army and used by Gen Joseph Galliéni to ferry troops from Paris to the Battle of the Marne.*

The scene was described by Private Edward Roe:

'At 3 am we move off. Great difficulty moving along owing to roads being congested with refugees... Next morning we pick up some fifty men of the Lancashire Fusiliers. All bear traces of the previous day's fighting and seem thoroughly "done up". Some have rifles and no equipment, others part of their equipment and no rifles. German cavalry are pressing our rear and every available man has to fall in. We form a line in rear and flanks of the convoy. The convoy is saved as the French or Belgian cavalry regiment holds them back. The enemy has brought his artillery into action and shells are bursting perilously near. However, by assisting the exhausted horses and by much shouting and cracking of whips we manage to get wagons and limbers over the steep hill that confronted us and get out of one tight corner... Every hour we pick up stragglers of various units... It is impossible to identify one Regiment from another as all cap badges, numerals or titles have been given away as souvenirs... Dead horses, sides of beef, boxes of milk, tea, jam; "bully" [beef] and biscuits mark our line of retreat.'

All this delayed German victory, frustrations being compounded by knowledge that but five weeks had been allowed for the campaign in the west, and that already Russian armies had entered East Prussia. The war in Belgium was getting serious. In 1915 the British government Bryce Committee on Alleged German Outrages concluded that there were 'deliberate and organised massacres', murder, looting, and burnings, 'the rules and usages of war' being 'frequently broken'. Whilst the 'Rape of Belgium' was over-reported—probably wilfully exaggerated at the time— it was real. Exactitude is illusive but it appears that in some cases at least 'friendly fire' incidents between German units were interpreted as the actions of *franc-tireurs* and the reaction was paranoid and draconian. Tamines and Dinant suffered particularly.

At Leuven *Infanterie Regiment Nr 84* reported coming under fire, from, it was claimed, members of the Civil Guard out of uniform, and in immediate response what were euphemistically described as 'strict

Original Aufnahme vom Kriegsschauplatz.
Das einsame Grab eines Garde Dragoners
auf dem Fort Loucin bei Lüttich; der Tapfere
fiel bei dem Versuch, die erste Fahne aufzupflanzen.

Kr. 75
Verlag von
GUSTAV LIERSCH & Cº
BERLIN S.W.

Above: *A posed photograph showing German trench fighters in the latter part of the war. The weapons shown include G98 Mauser rifles, stick grenades, and a captured Maxim machine gun. The figure to the right observes using a trench periscope camouflaged with sandbag fabric.*

Opposite: *Poppies on the battlefield of Le Cateau. After Mons the British army scuttled back across the border into France in an exhausting fighting retreat. At Le Cateau on 26 August 1914 the BEF turned and fought a delaying action before again withdrawing on St Quentin.*

measures' were invoked. The *New York Tribune* reporter described an orgy of destruction:

'On Tuesday evening a body of German troops who had been driven back retired in disorder upon the town of Louvain. Germans who were guarding the town thought that the retiring troops were Belgians and fired upon them. In order to excuse this mistake the Germans, in spite of the most energetic denials on the part of the authorities, pretended that Belgians had fired on the Germans, although all the inhabitants, including policemen, had been disarmed for more than a week. Without any examination and without listening to any protest the commanding officer announced that the town would be immediately destroyed. All inhabitants had to leave their homes at once; some were made prisoners; women and children were put into a train of which the destination was unknown; soldiers with fire bombs set fire to the different quarters of the town; the splendid Church of St. Pierre, the markets, the university and its scientific establishments, were given to the flames, and it is probable that the Hotel de Ville, this celebrated jewel of Gothic art, will also have disappeared in the disaster. Several notabilities were shot at sight. Thus a town of 40,000 inhabitants, which, since the fifteenth century, has been the intellectual and scientific capital of the Low Countries, is a heap of ashes. Americans, many of whom have followed the course at this illustrious alma mater and have there received such cordial hospitality, cannot remain insensible to this outrage on the rights of humanity and civilization which is unprecedented in history.'

More than 200 civilians died at Leuven. Total executions in Belgium ran into four figures, in addition to those many civilians who became the collateral damage of bombardment and battle. A million citizens fled as refugees, taking with them vivid impressions of terror.

Opposite, below: *Graves of men of the Chinese Labour Corps, Lijssenthoek Military Cemetery. Inaugurated in 1916 the corps was recruited for non-combatant duties, and by the end of the following year more than 50,000 were serving in France. Though some were killed by shelling or died by other causes, the 35 buried at Lijssenthoek all died in 1919, probably as a result of the Spanish Influenza which swept Europe in the wake of war. The gravestones are of standard British and Commonwealth shape, but have names inscribed in Chinese characters and a motto in English, as for example, 'A Good Reputation Endures Forever'.*

Below right: *A German advertisement for one of the many new gadgets needed with the onset of static warfare, the 'trench periscope'. In this example the device concertinas and folds flat when the mirrors are closed.*

Meanwhile the German field armies pushed remorselessly forward, but, in deviation from their original plan, struck east of Paris chasing the apparently defeated British, with hopes of rolling up the French forces from their left flank. This proved to be a serious mistake, for though the French army had already suffered losses, the notoriously unflappable Marshal Joseph Joffre, French Commander in Chief, was able to take measures to rebalance his forces to face the threat. The result was the titanic clash of the battle of the Marne, commencing on 5 September. What gave the French a vital edge was the commitment of a new Sixth Army under the 67-year old General Michel-Joseph Manoury against the German right wing. The British now also rejoined the action. On a battlefront of a hundred miles half a dozen armies on either side now fought a battle that might have decided the war.

With the halting of the German offensive on the Marne, and the subsequent Anglo-French counterstroke attempted on the Aisne, both sides consolidated their fronts: initially with simple trenches and pits, later with ever more sophisticated works. Strategically the only option appeared to be to outflank these new obstacles to the north: and so began the so-called 'race to the sea' in which, one after another, opposing armies attempted to get around an ever-lengthening defensive line. After the fall of Antwerp on 9 October additional German forces were released, and reinforcement also began to arrive in the shape of the BEF, which was redirected back northwards to Belgium. Belgian defence then rested on the River Yser, where trenchant defence with the assistance of French Marines and Territorials only narrowly prevented a serious breakthrough during the battle which opened on 16 October. After repeated attempts the sluice gates at Nieuwpoort were opened at the end of the month by engineer Hendrik Geeraert, inundating an already low-lying and boggy terrain, and an attempted German breakthrough at Ramskappelle was halted. The Western Front now extended for about 450 miles, resting solidly on both the Alps and the English Channel. There were no flanks, and nowhere on that front that could not be reached by shells.

Capt Noel Chavasse (1884–1917), RAMC

Chavasse is buried at Brandhoek New Military Cemetery between Poperinge and Ypres. The son of the bishop of Liverpool, he was the only soldier to win the VC twice during World War I. Attached to the Liverpool Scottish as a medical officer from 1913, he arrived in France in November 1914. Chevasse was awarded the MC for his conduct at Hooge in 1915, but his first VC was for rescuing and tending casualties under fire, close to the enemy trenches at Guillemont in August 1916, 'showing courage and self sacrifice beyond praise'. His second came at the beginning of the Third Battle of Ypres when he repeated his exploits, though himself injured. As his second citation reported:

'Though severely wounded early in the action whilst carrying a wounded soldier to the Dressing Station, Capt. Chavasse refused to leave his post, and for two days not only continued to perform his duties, but in addition went out repeatedly under heavy fire to search for and attend to the wounded who were lying out. During these searches, although practically without food during this period, worn with fatigue and faint with his wound, he assisted to carry in a number of badly wounded men, over heavy and difficult ground. By his extraordinary energy and inspiring example, he was instrumental in rescuing many wounded who would have otherwise undoubtedly succumbed under the bad weather conditions. This devoted and gallant officer subsequently died of his wounds.'

Dixmude

Below: *A covered bunker on the Boyau de la Mort, or Dodengang, on the left bank of the Yser, near Dixmude. Occupied by Belgian troops for most of the war, these defences began as shallow ditches, and were first dug on order of Gen Jacques as part of a tactical struggle to command the site of nearby oil tanks. Very quickly, however, fighting descended into an attritional struggle with several episodes of close-quarter battle, and the trenches were progressively deepened and reinforced to include bunkers, machine gun positions and the Mousetrap twin observation post.*

Right: *Initially preserved by the Touring Club of Belgium, and subsequently maintained by engineers of the Belgian Army, the Dixmude 'Trench of Death' was consolidated with cement as early as 1924. The site was formally adopted as an historic monument in 1992, and a museum here opened in 2004. In this view it can be seen that the main font line consists of a series of fire bays, behind which runs a supporting walkway.*

Above: *The ruins of Dixmude in winter. The town fell on 10 November 1914, and thereafter stood in the front lines until retaken in 1918. It was bombarded intermittently for the better part of four years. From a population of 3,884 in 1910, there were little over a thousand in Dixmude in 1920.*

Right: *Dixmude as it appears in the early 21st century, fully restored. St Nicholas Church was destroyed a second time in May 1940, and its present version dates from 1945. The town hall, which dates from 1428, had been modified over the centuries but after World War I was reconstructed in the style of the Flemish Renaissance.*

Above: *A German soldier smokes his pipe among the rubble of Dixmude. The town was first shelled on 16 October 1914, with infantry attacks commencing four days later, at which time the church was smashed with heavier projectiles. Among the defenders were French Marines, one of whom reported that, 'the noise was stupendous', with '420mm, 305mm and 77mm [guns] thundering in unison'. When the enemy attacked they were met by close-range machine gun fire. Soon, however, the entire quarter about the church was in flames.*

1

2

A

'Toc H'

Toc H, more properly known as Talbot House, opened at Poperinge in December 1915. Toc H was a church club established by Army Chaplain P.B. 'Tubby' Clayton (1885–1972), on the orders of his senior Chaplain Neville Talbot. The house chosen (**1**) was that of a local hop merchant, monsieur Camerlynk, but the name was chosen in honor of Neville's brother, Lt Gilbert W.L. Talbot, 7th Battalion, Rifle Brigade, son of the Bishop of Winchester. He was just 23 when killed in heavy fighting at Hooge on 30 July 1915, but it was not possible to recover his body for a week. He is buried in Sanctuary Wood Cemetery (**2**), his grave at **A**. There were originally three cemeteries in this vicinity, all established in the summer of 1915, but two were later obliterated in the battle of Mount Sorrell. The remaining cemetery, redesigned by Sir Edwin Lutyens after the war, was much expanded to almost 2,000 interments by bringing together graves from other cemeteries.

Although Toc H grew into an international Christian movement in the interwar period, during the war Clayton did not labour the religious nature of the establishment that he was pleased to call 'Everyman's Club'. All ranks were welcome and the facilities included a library, piano and canteen. After the war Toc H was again reopened as a hostel and remains one of the most interesting and authentic places to stay on the Western Front. Clayton was born in Australia of English parents. He studied theology at Exeter College, Oxford, and worked as a curate before going to the front as a chaplain. A life-size model (**3**) of him stands in the entrance to the museum, which is located in the hop store in the garden. He had his own room in Toc H (**5**), and like much of the house this has been refurbished with period artefacts—some original to Toc H. In the attic is a chapel (**4**) which contains the original grave marker of Gilbert Talbot (**B** and **inset**), a comparatively recent addition, having been anonymously donated in the 1990s. The General's Room is decorated with an original sketch by Eric Kennington (1888–1960), himself an infantryman before being engaged as a war artist in 1917.

3

Top: *Located by a small stream on the edge of Ploegsteert Wood, Mud Corner cemetery was designed by G.H. Goldsmith and contains just 84 burials. The cemetery was opened in June 1917, and the dead served with New Zealand and Australian forces. In this view the larger Prowse Point Cemetery can also be seen on the horizon. This was named after Brig Charles Prowse, formerly of the Somerset Light Infantry, who fell on the first day of the Somme.*

Above: *The mossy remains of bunkers deep in Ploegsteert Wood. Captured by British cavalry in October 1914, it was later partially taken back by the Germans. They were pushed out again, only to return during the Spring Offensive of 1918. Today the trees have grown back, but in places the ground is shell-pocked and both British and German fortifications survive. The small cemeteries in the wood are Rifle House, Hyde Park Corner, Toronto Avenue and Ploegsteert Wood.*

Right: *The Ploegsteert Memorial to the Missing commemorates 11,387 officers and men with no known grave, lost on the fields of battle that straddle the Franco-Belgian border. The monument stands on the edge of Berks Cemetery Extension, a burial ground first opened in 1916, but much expanded in 1930 by the consolidation of burials from other sites. A Last Post ceremony is conducted at the memorial once a month.*

Chapter 2
The First and Second Battles of Ypres

...N WILHELM KRIEGSFREIWILLIGER † 24.4.1915 ...
G-KARL MUSKETIER † 4.10.1917 · RETTER STEFAN
RIEGSFREIWILLIGER † 31.10.1914 · RETTIG ALBERT
NFANTERIST † 26.4.1918 · REUFER JOHANNES R...ER
...VIST † 12.11.1914 · REUSCH AUGUST ERSATZ-RES...
17.6.1915 · REUSCHER WALTER RESERVIST † 12.10.191...
REUSS EDMUND MUSKETIER † 29.10.1914 · REUSS G...
N SCHÜTZE † 5.5.1918 · REUSS LUITPOLD INFANTE...
5.7.1916 · REUTER HERMANN GEFREITER † 25.9.1917
11.1914 · REUTER KARL HAUPTMANN † 2.12.1914 · RE...
L MUSKETIER † 19.10.1918 · REUTHER ADAM KRANK...
T UNTEROFFIZIER † 2.11.1914 · REUTZSCH ALFRED W...
ST † 20.11.1914 · REYHER WILHELM ERSATZ-RESERVI...
GEORG LANDSTURMMANN † 7.11.1917 · RICH JOHANN
...6.8.1914 · RICHARDT ALBERT † 8.1914 · RICHARDT...
...STIAN LANDSTURMMANN † 12.10.1917 · RICHTER EMIL
...EITER † 23.8.1914 · RICHTER FRITZ LEUTNANT † 1.11.191...
CHTER HANS GEFREITER † 31.10.1914 · RICHTER HAN...
R † 5.7.1917 · RICHTER KURT VIZEFELDWEBEL † 28.1.191...
...4.5.1915 · RICHTER OSKAR ERSATZ-RESERVIST † 9.2.19...
RICHTER OTTO RESERVIST † 26.8.1914 · RICHTER REINH...
RICHTER PAUL SOLDAT † 31.10.1914 · RICHTER...
...RICHTER PAUL SOLDAT † 22.8.1914 · RICHTER SOLDAT · RICHTER
...RT RESERVIST † 22.8.1914 · RICHTER SOLDAT † 13.4.1915
...29.10.1914 · RICKEN HARTWICH WEHRMANN † 26.9.1...
...GER † 30.4.1918 · RICKLE WILLIBALD GEFREITER † RIECHERS H...
OHANN ERSATZ-RESERVIST † 29.10.1914 · RIEDEL GUSTAV ERSATZ-R...
...ANN RESERVIST † 26.8.1914 · RIEDEL KARL SOLDAT † 13.5.1915
...RIEDEL KARL SOLDAT † 5.10.1917 · RIE...
...TERIST † 4.11.1917 · RIEDER KONRAD INFANTERIST † 12.11...
...19.7 · RIEDER FRIEDRICH INFANTERIST † 14.11.1914 · RIE...
...2.1917 · RIEDINGER FRIEDRICH INFANTERIST † 14.11.1914 · RIEDM...
...RIEDL LUDWIG INFANTERIST † 25.10.1914 · RI...
...7.7.1917 · RIEDMÜLLER EMIL MUSKETIER † 24.5.1918 · RI...
...RIEDMÜLLER EMIL MUSKETIER · RIEGER AN...
...RIEDT JOHANNES VIZEFELDWEBEL † 17.12.1914 · RIEGER...
...RESERVIST · RIEGER FRIEDRICH...

Previous page: *Langemarck German Cemetery, see also pp68–69.*

Opposite: *Memorial crosses tucked into the reinforcing rods of a concrete bunker atop Hill 60. The compulsion to make personal tributes remains immensely strong amongst modern visitors—unfortunately so does the desire to take souvenirs or 'embellish' the battlefields. Visitor books and dedicated walls may help to channel such impulses into forms that do not adversely affect the landscape.*

Below: *At the second battle of Ypres, the Germans used Chlorine gas for the first time on the Western Front. It led to panic in the British lines although the Germans were unable to exploit their tactical success thanks to the swift arrival of the Canadian reserves.*

For the British, Canadians, and Belgians few cities can have as much resonance as the medieval cloth town of Ypres; in World War I the most significant place remaining in the last sliver of unoccupied Belgium. Yet the holding of what the Tommies soon knew as 'Wipers' was no foregone conclusion, for given a fair choice no general in his right mind would have attempted to have held such a precarious salient, overlooked by low hills, from which the enemy could not only bombard with his artillery but actually see the spires of the town from his vantage points. As modern visitors will appreciate terms such as 'hill' and 'ridge' are relative in this context, the Passchendaele Ridge, for example, being a mere 70ft (21m) above the surrounding plain: the Messines Ridge reached about 150ft (46m). Hill 60, as its name suggests, rested on the 60-metre (196ft) contour line of the map, though it was in reality a man-made spoil heap created by the excavation of a railway cutting. Nevertheless, Ypres blocked the way to the all-important Channel ports, served as a potential jumping off point for new British armies, and fulfilled the pledge that the British Empire had entered this war to save Belgium.

British involvement here began optimistically, with Ferdinand Foch, French commander in the north, encouraging an immediate advance on Menin in order to turn what was perceived as the enemy flank: but the Germans had other ideas. For in the latter part of October 1914 they struck towards the city, opening what would later become known as the First Battle of Ypres. Though regular British infantry bore the brunt, the Indian Corps, which had arrived at Marseilles on 30 September, formed an immediate reserve, and cavalry were used to hold parts of the front-line trenches. Territorials had also begun to arrive, with the London Scottish first into action holding Messines Ridge. The French came in to hold the northern sector.

Private Edward Roe of the East Lancashires faced the enemy attack on 2 November:

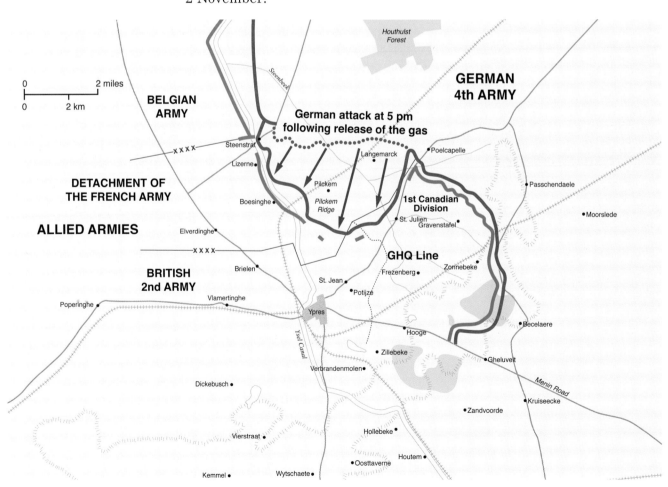

The bombardment was heavier than usual. The German shells blew the tobacco leaves, ground sheets and doors off the top of our dugouts… The morning mist lifted and revealed to our gaze lines and lines of solid grey advancing. Our gunners have spotted them… tearing gaps in the closely packed German lines. Bandoliers of ammunition are feverishly passed down the trench line. Our two Maxims are on them. Captain Clayhills, DSO restrains us from firing until they get within 500 yards of our line. They are advancing with the utmost confidence. "Now let them have it!" and we did. We are reloading and firing like mad; still the advance continues. Our rifles get jammed with clay. With utmost persuasion and much swearing we can only average about eight rounds per rifle per minute. We take our bolts out of our rifles and urinate on them, as we have no rifle oil. Our batteries in the rear are sending over a continuous stream of shells…'

The climax of the battle came on 11 November with the Prussian Guard and supporting divisions attacking just north of the Menin Road, a bare four miles from the centre of Ypres. The British were nearly broken, but saved, so the legend goes, by the sending to the line of every last man. This has basis in fact, for as the regimental chronicles of the Oxfordshire and Buckinghamshire Light Infantry reported, a brigade of artillery had found itself exposed to attack through Nonne Bosschen wood. Its adjutant therefore pushed into the line a scratch force of 'gunners, cooks etc', armed with rifles, to keep the Germans away from the guns and vulnerable equipment until help, in the form of the 2nd Ox and Bucks, could make its appearance. That battalion's commander, Lt-Col Davies, was at the moment under orders to retake another position, but apprehending the peril rapidly changed his plans:

Below: *The Ypres cloth hall or Lakenhalle at Christmas. Originally erected as a market and store for woollen cloth, it was completed in 1304, but was almost obliterated during World War I.' After the war the building underwent lengthy restoration by architects Coomans and Pauwels. The once modest museum here has been dramatically improved over the years becoming the Salient Museum, and later the remarkable In Flanders Fields, itself refitted and reopened in 2012 ready for the centenary.*

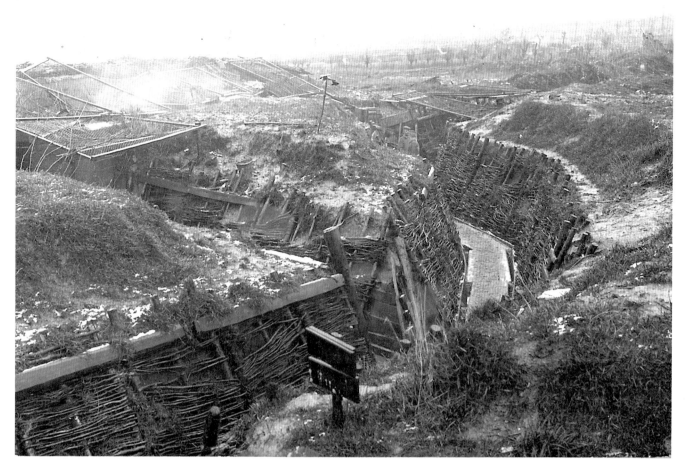

'It was obvious that the Germans must be cleared out of Nonne Bosschen, as they were here in dangerous proximity to some of our guns and some French guns... I sent A and B companies... this they did most successfully, driving the Germans before them, and killing and capturing a good many. C and D companies followed in support. When A and B came out on the south-eastern edge of the wood they were joined by the Northamptonshire on the right, and by some Connaught Rangers and Sappers on the left... They charged the Germans out of the trenches, some of the enemy turning and running when the attack was 30 or 40 yards off, and others surrendering. Most of those who ran were shot. The men with whom we had this fight were the Potsdam Guards. They were very fine, big men, but by the time we came across them they did not seem to have much fight in them, as they had been under our artillery for some time, and this, no doubt, had shaken them considerably.'

For the Germans the bloody First Ypres created a yet more powerful legend, the *Kindermord zu Ypren*, or 'Massacre of the Innocents' at Ypres. A German High Command communiqué, widely reported in home newspapers, made reference to attacks 'West of Langemarck' in which 'young regiments singing *Deutschland über Alles* broke forward against the front lines of the enemy's position and took them.' The 'young regiments' mentioned were the troops of four new Reserve Corps which had arrived in Belgium as recently as the second week of October. Though actually a mixture of experienced reservists and volunteers, there were many school leavers, students, and teachers in the ranks. These formations did indeed fall enthusiastically upon the enemy, with little heed for any tactical nicety, and were met with machine guns and rapid rifle fire. As Capt C.J. Paterson of the South Wales Borderers put it, the 'silly idiots' came on in 'great masses'. The resultant losses were little short of catastrophic. Over

the course of the battle each of the four corps suffered upwards of 10,000 casualties. In certain units the losses were proportionately greater, with *Reserve Infanterie Regiment Nr 208*, for example, down to just 16 officers out of an original 60, and 213 men out of 2,750 still fit for service.

Many aspects of the story of the *Kindermord* have been questioned, and the 'myth of Langemarck' was very much exploited in later years, but the idea that the young reservists sang as they went into battle appears plausible. Various reports of 1914 speak of troops singing, not only on the march, but in the attack, though such vocalisation was not just bravado, being also intended to raise morale, and to identify friendly forces under conditions of poor visibility. Capt Glazebrook of the Gloucesters recalled the enemy 'singing patriotic songs' as they advanced; another German report spoke of *Reserve Infanterie Regiment Nr 204* singing both the song destined to become the national anthem after the war and *Die Wacht am Rhein* in the rain at Dixmude by way of recognition signal.

Though fighting continued until late November the line stabilised with the British still in control of Ypres, if very tightly hemmed about by the enemy around Sanctuary Wood and Nonne Bosschen. Conditions were primitive that winter, as one eyewitness of the 20th Hussars recalled of the scene near Kemmel:

'It is interesting to note that although these trenches were so close to the Germans, there were no communication trenches. We just walked straight into the front line over the top, and this on a frosty night with snow on the ground that cracked violently under our feet. Yet relief took place without our being in any way disturbed by the enemy. These trenches, which had been made by the French, were provided with "overhead cover". All firing was done through loopholes. There was very little wire, and I think the position would easily have been rushed by a surprise assault... We remained in the trenches all the 22nd, a lovely bright frosty day. There was a good bit of sniping on both sides, and the Huns shelled us at times with "Black Marias" [heavy shells bursting in a cloud of smoke].'

Whilst the British moved a little way south, experiencing the remarkable if surreal Christmas Truce of 1914 in the Armentières sector, they would be back around Ypres by April 1915, together with the Canadians and French colonial troops, just in time to experience a new and yet more

Opposite: *The Canadian memorial at Vancouver Corner, St Julien. Over 30ft (10m) tall the 'brooding soldier' was designed by Frederick Chapman Clemesha, who was himself wounded serving with the Canadian Corps. The figure holds his rifle muzzle down, as in mourning. The monument was unveiled in 1923. An inscription states that, 'This Column Marks the Battlefield where 18,000 Canadians on the British left withstood the first German gas attacks of 22nd–24th April. 2,000 fell and here lie buried.'*

Below: *The solid granite-block Canadian memorial at Hill 62 commemorating actions at this location, and at Mount Sorrel, St Eloi and other locations in the southern part of the salient during the spring and summer of 1916.*

St George's

An Anglican church for Ypres was planned as early as 1919, donations being solicited by FM French during the early 1920s. After Lord French died in 1925 it was furtherplanned that the church should also be a memorial to him. Lord Plumer laid the foundation stone in July 1927, and St George's, designed by Sir Reginald Blomfield, was finally consecrated on 24 June 1929, by the Bishop of Fulham. It has wonderful stained-glass windows (Opposite) dedicated to the Household Brigade and Guards Division. The windows were made by the London firm of Clayton and Bell, the designs being attributed to Reginald Bell. Other lights commemorate other units and individual officers, including the Grenfell brothers who served with the 9th Lancers, Capt Boyce Combe and the Australian Capt Loftus Jones. A bust sculpted by American Jo Davidson (1883–1952) commemorates Lord French. There is also a remarkable collection of hassocks (Below). The four in the foreground symbolise (L–R) the forces of Australia, New Zealand, Canada and South Africa. In the row behind are three to the Royal Fusiliers.

terrible expression of modern war. For many Entente troops the first realisation that a second battle of Ypres had started was the appearance of a greenish-yellow cloud on the afternoon of 22 April 1915. The French Moroccans and Algerians soon realised that this was no ordinary smoke and ran choking from their trenches, or died at their posts. As Capt Hugh Pollard, VC, observed:

'One cannot blame them that they broke and fled. In the gathering dark of that awful night they fought with the terror, running blindly in the gas-cloud, and dropping with breasts heaving in agony and the slow poison of suffocation mantling their dark faces. Hundreds of them fell and died; others lay helpless, froth upon their agonized lips and their racked bodies powerfully sick, with tearing nausea at short intervals. They too would die later—a slow and lingering death of agony unspeakable. The whole air was tainted with the acrid smell of chlorine that caught at the back of men's throats and filled their mouths with its metallic taste'.

All that stood in the way between the Germans and significant breakthrough was the Canadians, whose initial 1st Division front line had stretched from the vicinity of Gravenstafel, round to join the French flank on the Poelcapelle road. Now they had to shift briskly to their left, contracting the front and blocking the gap left by the French. Nevertheless the enemy managed to get a lodgement across the Ypres canal. Local counterattacks, reinforced by the British, continued long into the night. Battle continued on 24 April with further releases of gas against the Canadians at St Julien. The Germans, who had originally viewed their limited offensive as a local distraction from events on the Eastern Front and a large scale trial with a new weapon, were surprised by developments and ill-prepared to capitalise on first success. Nevertheless battle was repeatedly renewed into May with the British, now under the steady and reliable, if cautious, hand of Gen Herbert 'Daddy' Plumer, forced to make withdrawals to secure the front and economise on men. Eventually the line stabilised. There was an alarmingly large dent in the salient, with Langemarck and Pilckem now in enemy hands, but again Ypres was held.

What was really shocking about the debut of gas was not that men died, but the way they died—or continued to live. Lt-Col G.W.G. Hughes recalled:

'I shall never forget the sights I saw up by Ypres after the first gas attack. Men lying all along the side of the road between Poperinghe and Ypres, exhausted, gasping, frothing yellow mucus from their mouths, their faces blue and distressed. It was dreadful and so little could be done for them. One came away from seeing or treating them longing to be able to go straight away at the Germans and throttle them, to pay them out in some sort of way for their devilishness. Better for a sudden death than this awful agony.'

GUARDS DIVISION • ROYAL ARTILLERY • BRIGADE OF GUARDS • ROYAL ENGINEERS • GUARDS DIVISION

1ST LIFE GUARDS • 2ND LIFE GUARDS • ROYAL HORSE GUARDS • GUARDS MACHINE GUN REGIMENT

DIEU ET MON DROIT

ROYAL ARMS

GRENADIER GUARDS • SCOTS GUARDS • WELSH GUARDS • IRISH GUARDS • COLDSTREAM GUARDS

TO THE GLORY OF GOD AND IN MEMORY OF ALL RANKS OF THE HOUSEHOLD BRIGADE AND THE GUARDS DIVISION WHO GAVE THEIR LIVES IN THE GREAT WAR 1914-18

Nevertheless gas was an unpredictable weapon, blown hither and yon by wind, killing some, permanently disabling others and temporarily incapacitating many. L/Cpl Jim Keddie, serving with the Canadians, was one of those who got a very frightening whiff of chlorine at the Second Ypres, but not enough to put him out of action. It made his eyes smart and run and he became 'violently sick', but it 'passed off fairly soon'. Gas had arrived, soon filling a niche as an area weapon: dreadful, but imprecise, and not by itself a battle winner especially as all sides looked for ways to protect themselves. Handkerchiefs doused with water, or better, urine, quickly gave way to pads and primitive masks. These were superseded by hood-like 'gas helmets' on the British side, and the Germans produced a quite modern-looking mask with detachable filter by late 1915. Later in the war the British and the Americans would use a very effective Small Box Respirator, though proper protection depended upon being able to get the device on in double-quick time. Doing so was aided by sentries whose job it was to sound a bell or horn, beat an old shell case, or otherwise raise the alarm.

Right: *The view from the tower of the Cloth Hall looking out across the town square and a temporary volleyball court, eastward towards the Menin Gate (A). This view emphasises the low ridge occupied by the Germans for much of the war, dominating the strategic situation. Zonnebeke lies approximately straight ahead, Langemarck off to the left, and Gueveld somewhere off to the right. Orientation from the British perspective was arguably more difficult than from the German, since the latter generally occupied higher ground, and had the landmark of Ypres to gauge distance and direction. After three years, three battles and many minor engagements the Germans were eventually forced back about six miles from this point. Ypres was held: but the cost of fighting here, to the British Empire in general, was gargantuan.*

Though the Ypres front now reached a sort of equilibrium and no major offensive would be made in the West by the Germans until 1916, it would be wrong to think of pretty well any part of the salient as a 'quiet sector'. Topography, and a situation with the enemy on three sides, ensured little rest from shelling, sniping, and raids. Moreover, serious fighting broke out again later in May with the Germans attacks from Frezenberg and at Bellewaarde ridge where there were actions in both May and September. In July at Hooge the enemy deployed flamethrowers. Almost every yard of the salient would be bombarded, fought over, fortified, dug, or otherwise impacted by war, and names like 'Hellfire Corner', 'Shrapnel Corner', and 'Shell Trap Farm' were chosen with good reason.

Shell Trap Farm, later rechristened 'Mouse Trap Farm', perhaps for reasons of morale, lay in the front lines near St Julien, and was occupied by 1st East Lancashires in May 1915. The place was described with a cynical sarcasm by Private Edward Roe:

continued on page 65

Hooge

The lake at Hooge crater (**Above**), created by a British mine blast, is one of the most interesting places in the salient today, lying within yards of not only Hooge Crater Cemetery, but a packed museum, recently re-excavated trenches and German bunkers. The building in the background is the Hotel Kasteel, in the rebuilt stable block once serving the Hooge Chateau.

The two photos at right show (**Above right**) a German bunker at Hooge dating to 1916 with, in the background left, two Livens projector barrels. The interior of the same bunker (**Below right**) in 2013 shows the water has been pumped out and the soil removed. Electric lighting reveals the structure of blocks and rods and the use of steel in the roof. The re-excavated trench at Hooge (**Opposite**) gives some impression of how Flanders trenches might appear in bad weather and without pumping out.

'The farm is surrounded by a moat, dead Jerries and British soldiers lie about. Truly a cheerful-looking place. We push on and occupy a line of trenches beyond the moated farm and breastwork without opposition. Dawn has broken and a few Germans are dodging about 200 yards in front. No firing has taken place up to the present. Our new line trenches stench abominably. One encounters or feels a springy feeling underneath the feet when walking along the trench floor. Of course we are walking on the bodies of men who have been buried there at an earlier date. Patches of field grey (German), khaki (British), and horizon blue (French) cloth show, or appear behind a thin film of clay, on the trench parapet and parados. The ground in front and rear is seared with shell craters of huge dimensions. The trench is filled in places by the action of high explosive shells. The moated, or "Shell Trap" farm is no more, or at least not until it has been rebuilt. Broken rifles, bayonets, and equipment strew the ground everywhere. The owners of the same are just buried, or a layer of clay scraped over them, on the lips of shell craters or the trench parapet or parados. In some cases they were dumped into dugouts, the dugouts were then undermined and allowed to fall on the dead. It simplified grave digging; in fact I don't suppose there was any time to dig graves. I counted fifteen dead and bloated figures in service dress lying on the embankment of the moat to our rear left.'

Essex Farm

The Essex Farm Cemetery **(Opposite)** *was established on the canal bank by a dressing station near the front line in 1915 and remained in use until 1917. There are 1,200 servicemen buried or commemorated, and in this view can also be seen the 49th Division Memorial. One of the best-known graves, so frequently visited by school parties that nearby grass has been worn away and replaced with artifical turf, is that of Valentine J. Strudwick of Dorking. Aged just 14, Strudwick joined the 8th Battalion, Rifle Brigade, and was 15 when killed in January 1916. The bunkers of Essex Farm dressing station* **(Below).** *It was here that Lt-Col John Mcrae, a Canadian doctor, composed the poem In Flanders Fields in 1915. At the end of the war the work, with its evocation of wind-blown poppies, prompted American academic Moina Michael to suggest the adoption of this flower as a general symbol of remembrance.*

Sanctuary Wood

Sanctuary Wood was so named when the sector was relatively quiet: it was not so for long. In 1918 the site was almost devoid of trees, and revetments have been replaced more than once in the last century. Today, there are preserved British trenches and shellholes **(Left and Below left).** *In one corner of the site are fragments of broken German gravestones from men killed early in the war. There are large and eclectic collections at Sanctuary Wood. Items in this area include a German trench mortar, shells, trench armour, and rifles* **(Below).** *A collection of debris from the battlefield—along with animal bones, wheels, fragments of trees and shells can be seen a couple of less obvious items. The rusted rolls are unused barbed wire; the rods with spiral points, to the right, are barbed wire picquets. Metal picquets were preferable to wooden stakes, not only because they were lighter and less bulky, but because they could be screwed quietly into the ground avoiding enemy attention.*

Langemarck German Cemetery

The cemetery was created around bunkers and holds well over 44,000 dead: by 1984 research had revised the cumulative total upward to 44,294; as of 2013 the Volksbund Deutsche Kriegsgräberfürsorge cites a figure of 44,304. The entrance building at the cemetery has a chapel-like room with oak panels inscribed with the 6,313 known names of the 10,143 soldiers who were originally buried in the lower part of the cemetery.

About 3,000 of the graves at Langemarck were those of young student volunteers killed in October and November 1914, during the First Battle of Ypres. As a result the cemetery became known as the Student Cemetery.

At Langemarck, memorials to specific units take the form of sarcophagi. Casting the name of the deceased in bronze, with rank and date of death in relief, is the typical German manner of commemorating those interred in mass graves (see chapter opening photo). A couple of British dead are included on other tablets here.

Many German World War I cemeteries lacked embellishment until after 1945, so many of the features we see today are relatively recent, including an audiovisual interepretation alongside the cemetery.

The period German postcards show:
*(**1**) Langemarck in 1915, 'destroyed by the enemy'. By 1918 there would be almost nothing recognisable.*

*(**2**) Captured trenches, 23 April 1915. Though the caption refers to 'English' trenches the wicker gabions and soldiers' uniforms suggest they were French.*

*(**3**) Captured enemy trenches on 22 April 1915, the day the Second Battle of Ypres commenced. These shelters are not shell-proof and deep excavation was made difficult by a high water table. Interestingly, scruffy sandbags were better than neatly topped walls over which the appearance of a human form was more obvious.*

Right and Opposite: *Langemarck cemetery showing the mass grave and flat memorial tablets. The three small crosses are a symbol frequently used by the German War Graves Commission. The concrete bunkers were intensively constructed around the salient from the midwar period, making attack extremely difficult. Many bunkers lacked forward-facing embrasures, the intention being maximum protection, the occupants rushing out to defend shell holes and trenches when bombardment ceased.*

Chapter 3
The Third Battle of Ypres

Previous page: *The Menin Gate, see also pp86-87.*

Opposite: *Flying the Irish tricolour, the memorial to L/Cpl Francis Ledwidge, Royal Inniskilling Fusiliers (1887–1917). The poet's memorial is located close to the monument to the French colonial troops killed in the first major gas attack in 1915. Ledwidge was one of a group of men hit by a shell on the opening day of the Third Ypres, 1917.*

Below: *The movement of the line from its position on the day before the first attack at Messines on 7 June until the battle ended in the rain on 10 November after half a million men had become casualties.*

By mid-1917 the world had changed dramatically, even if the front around Ypres remained much where it had been more than a year earlier. Robert Nivelle's offensive had fallen apart the spring, taking with it not only its author, who was rapidly redeployed, but much of the French confidence. Mutinies followed. Russia was now teetering gradually towards the edge of oblivion: the offensive ordered by War Minister Alexander Kerensky collapsed in mid-July. Italy had now been battering away at the Austrians on the Isonzo for the better part of two years, but had made little visible progress through mountainous terrain. True, America had recently entered the war, but it would be another year before her armies were trained and armed, and at the Western Front in strength. In such circumstances there remained only one country that could presently pick up the burden of the war, and by confronting the Germans head on, hope to prevent a general disintegration of the Allied cause. There may have been better methods of greater subtlety, but what followed could scarcely be ignored.

The British plan was not supposed to be 'yet another' Ypres, but what actually was intended remains open to some debate. The uncharitable have suggested it was an offensive to end the war before the Americans could intervene; others that it was the offensive that made the war long enough that they would have time to arrive. It became a battle of attrition, but was advanced as a scheme of serious strategic purpose. Specifically it was a performance in three movements. In the preamble the enemy were to be blown, quite literally, off Messines ridge. Thus would they be denied at a stroke both observation and the ability to fire *en enfilade* across the salient. With attention focused on Messines approximately 3,000 guns would be moved up to hurl almost five tons of shells at every yard of the German lines, before a massive advance on a broad front to the north broke the tyranny of the salient for good. German rail connections would

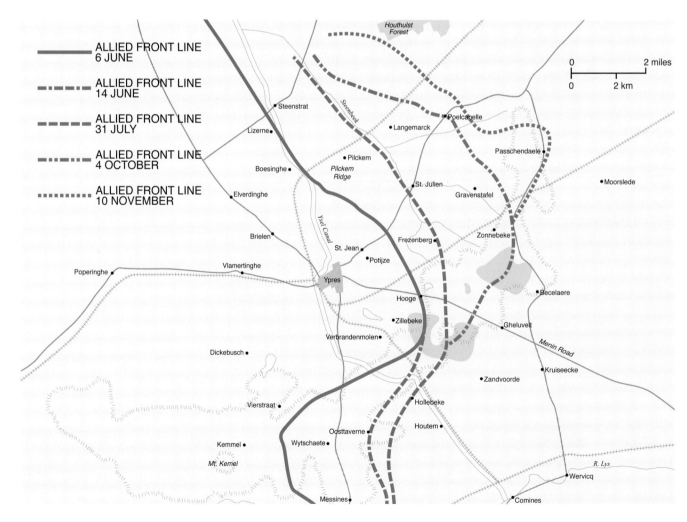

ALLIED FRONT LINE
6 JUNE

ALLIED FRONT LINE
14 JUNE

ALLIED FRONT LINE
31 JULY

ALLIED FRONT LINE
4 OCTOBER

ALLIED FRONT LINE
10 NOVEMBER

Above: *The farm known to the troops as Cheddar Villa also accommodated this large German bunker, one of many in this area. Cheddar Villa was taken on the opening day of the Third Ypres, and the bunker occupied by the Oxford and Buckinghamshire Light Infantry. Unfortunately an enemy shell flew straight into the opening, with predictable results.*

Right: *German troops relax in a concrete reinforced trench. Cement, much of it barged to the battlefront along inland waterways, made a major contribution to the German defence lines. It was used for reinforcing short sections of trench, and 'hardening' entrances, existing structures and cellars, as well as for the construction of new bunkers.*

be severed. In the last movement the British army would advance to clear the Belgian coast as landings left the enemy entirely unbalanced, and with no option but to retire. Though Lloyd George has been portrayed as reluctant, the War Cabinet nevertheless approved the scheme, and once started Haig was neither countermanded nor dismissed.

The new attack plan got off to a good start. The artillery made productive use of the 144,000 tons of shells earmarked for the Messines operation, and would dispose much of it either for counter battery fire to neutralise German guns, or in support of the infantry advance. Once the initial barrage ended many of the enemy regained their positions, expecting no doubt to man their machine guns and destroy the attacking ranks: but just 20 minutes later, at 03:10 on 7 June, 19 of the 21 mines so painfully dug under the ridge exploded with a massive detonation, audible in London. The total weight of explosives deployed was approximately a million pounds, and the largest single mine in excess of 90,000lb. Gen Plumer's Second Army infantry went forward, following a creeping barrage, with the British supported by II Anzac Corps on their right. Moving so hard on

Kirche von Poelcapelle vom feindl. Feuer zerstört.

Above: *The battered church at Poelcappelle, seen in a German photograph prior to the Third Ypres. The caption states that it has been 'destroyed by enemy fire'. In addition to the British cemetery the village now has a tank memorial and a centenary project to build a replica tank.*

the heels of the pyrotechnic mayhem, losses were relatively modest by the standards of the day. German 204th Division was pushed promptly from the ridge. Fighting continued until 14 June, by which time the objectives were achieved, with Plumer resisting pressure to attempt to bite off more than he could comfortably hold without further logistical preparation.

Four days later began the preliminary bombardment for the main attack: 3,000 guns raining down a total of 4.5 million shells. This deluge of fire was demoralising, but on the downside any surprise quickly evaporated, and the German defence, relying on reinforced concrete bunkers, machine guns and artillery, though damaged, was not fatally crippled. The burden of the main attack fell upon Sir Hubert Gough's Fifth Army, supported on the right by Plumer, and by French forces on the left, opening at 03:50 on 31 July. Modest gains were made around Pilckem Ridge, but the heaviest rain for some years now turned the churned ground into a quagmire. Tanks sunk into the mud, and the only cover left to the attackers was waterlogged shell holes. Getting artillery, fresh water, and supplies across such a man made sea of devastation meant that the advance could not be resumed quickly, and it was not until mid-August the full power of the offensive could be refocused at Langemarck. Fierce fighting led to little gain but heavy casualties. One who fought here was Capt Geoffrey Dugdale:

'Every gun on the British front within a distance of 25 miles opened fire simultaneously. It is impossible to express in words the effect, it was stupendous. It was useless even to shout, the noise of the machine gun barrage drowned the noise of the massed artillery. It was shattering. A wall of shells fell in front over the brook, obliterating the landscape. We could see nothing beyond. We rose to our feet shaking the dirt from our uniforms... The Colonel waved us forward to cross the brook, which we found was bridged with duckboards. The Oxfords were attacking in front of us. They were held up by a machine-gun post. They crept round it... A long line of troops on either side of us stretched as far as we could see— masses of men. The barrage was standing in front of us; soon it would

IN MEMORY OF THE
THE GREAT WAR

AS IN LANDED
41ST INFANTRY BRIGADE
7TH KING'S ROYAL RIFLE CORPS
8TH KING'S ROYAL RIFLE CORPS
7TH RIFLE BRIGADE
8TH RIFLE BRIGADE

42ND INFANTRY BRIGADE
5TH OXFORD AND BUCKS LIGHT INFANTRY
5TH KING'S SHROPSHIRE LIGHT INFANTRY
9TH KING'S ROYAL RIFLE CORPS
9TH RIFLE BRIGADE

43RD INFANTRY BRIGADE
6TH SOMERSET LIGHT INFANTRY
6TH DUKE OF CORNWALL'S LIGHT INFANTRY
6TH KING'S OWN YORKSHIRE LIGHT INFANTRY
10TH DURHAM LIGHT INFANTRY

14TH LIGHT DIVISION
MCMXIV — MCMXVIII

IN FRANCE IN MAY MCMXV
D SQADRON 1/1ST DUKE OF LANCASTER'S OWN YEOMANRY
DIVISIONAL CYCLIST COMPANY
46TH 47TH 48TH & 49TH
BRIGADES ROYAL FIELD ARTILLERY

DIVISIONAL AMMUNITION COLUMN
61ST 62ND AND 89TH FIELD
COMPANIES ROYAL ENGINEERS
DIVISIONAL SIGNAL COMPANY
8TH MOTOR MACHINE GUN BATTERY
11TH KING'S LIVERPOOL REGIMENT

PIONEERS
DIVISIONAL TRAIN 100TH 101TH 102TH & 103TH
COMPANIES ROYAL ARMY SERVICE CORPS
42ND 43RD AND 44TH FIELD AMBULANCES
26TH MOBILE VETERINARY SECTION

1915
CE
RDE

1916
OOD

TTES

1917
L HILL
RIDGE

lift to go forward... German machine guns opened fire from a pillbox no one had observed. The troops on our left were mown down like corn, their casualties were frightful. We lay down the bullets whistling over our heads; it looked as though the attack would be held up... Colonel Wood made up his mind. Jumping to his feet, staff in hand, he waved his battalion forward with his bandana handkerchief; on each side the others followed his lead. The situation was saved. We found afterwards that the Oxfords had been compelled to go round their objectives and attack from the flanks, owing to the pillboxes.'

Though Langemarck was taken, at every move British successes were faced by counterattacks. Progress was slow and losses on both sides heavy. Some of the German counterattacks used flamethrowers, as described by Capt Philip Christison of 6th Battalion Cameron Highlanders:

'Our rifles and light machine guns were now useless, being gummed up with mud, and we had to hurl grenades and then use pick handles in close combat. One had no time to feel frightened it happened so quickly. I saw a large Hun about to aim his flamethrower in my direction and CSM Adams with great presence of mind fired his Verey [signal] pistol at the man. The round hit the flamethrower and with a scream the man collapsed in a sheet of flame. We beat off this counterattack and formed a line of section posts, under heavy shellfire on any dry areas we could find.'

On 25 August a frustrated Haig transferred responsibility for the offensive from Gough to Plumer. More artillery was piled onto the front, and Plumer prepared an apparently ponderous step by step strategy designed to shove the enemy back in four stages, consolidating each time. It was perhaps highly predictable, with German Staff officer Albrecht von Thaer describing proceedings as 'almost boring', but it was more effective and cost the enemy dear as counterattacks now tended to hit well prepared positions. On 20 September the Allies attacked on the Menin Road supported by 1,300 guns, dropping shells in a concentration more than twice as heavy as that first at the beginning of the battle, and by 26 September Polygon Wood was cleared.

Opposite, above: *The New Zealand memorial at Gravenstafel. This obelisk was unveiled by Sir James Allen in August 1924. The slight rise and fall of the ground around this vicinity scarcely cause a cyclist to change gear, making it difficult to appreciate accounts that speak of the advances here as movement across a series of 'spurs'. However, on a landscape devoid of trees, crops or buildings even very slight rises took on tactical significance.*

Opposite, below: *The 14th (Light) Division memorial, Zwarteleen, near Hill 60. A Kitchener division formed in August 1914, the 14th fought at Hooge, the Somme, Third Ypres and in the final campaigns of 1918. The memorial has been moved bodily to its currently location as a result of threat of subsidence.*

Below: *Archaeological discoveries at the substantial Memorial Museum Passchendaele 1917, Zonnebeke. The pieces shown here are surprisingly well preserved and constitute the typical accoutrements of a German soldier. In the foreground are ammo pouches; in the centre, folding cutlery, buttons, belt buckle and shaving equipment. In the background are a rifle, bayonet, and a gas mask filter.*

On 4 October Plumer attacked at Broodseinde, a tiny settlement that local lore has it was named 'bread's end', because it was here that the local baker's delivery round finished. The troops went forward on a broad 8.7-mile (14,000m) front, and as luck would have it, Australian troops chanced upon an enemy who had been preparing his own attack and run into bombardment at the worst possible moment. Amongst others German 4th Guard Division suffered heavily, the third time since June. Though now urged by others to 'exploit' an apparent opportunity, Plumer again decided to hold his ground fighting off the enemy attempts to oust him from a relative position of defensive advantage, rather than assault new enemy lines poorly prepared. Both Gough and Plumer had now begun to think that the Third Ypres should be ended, but at Haig's conference on 6 October the direction was that the fight should go on.

Thereafter the rains returned. On 9 October at Poelcappelle things got off to a poor start with an Australian attempt to raid Celtic Wood by way of diversion. Of 85 men who charged into the wood intent on bombing German dugouts, only 14 returned unwounded. The Germans had been reinforced, and promptly chased Lt Scott's raiding party back through the mire. The officers were all hit, and Sgt Cole killed as he fired the flare to signal retreat. The artillery of both sides attempted to lend support in the confusion. Of the Australians 37 were missing without trace. In the main

Above: *Livens projector barrels at Sanctuary Wood. The Livens 'gas projector' idea was a significant technological step forward, as multiple barrels with electronic ignition could dump large quantities of gas onto a target area in short order.*

Right: *German bunkers at Zillebeke pictured in the interwar period. Located just south east of Ypres Zillebeke was scene of repeated fighting from 1914 onward.*

Opposite: *Stacked shells at Sanctuary Wood. Most of those shown here are shrapnel rounds, which were designed to break open over the enemy, peppering them with fast-moving 'shrapnel balls'. The basic idea was perfected in the 1780s by Henry Shrapnel, but remained a highly effective anti-personnel weapon against troops in the open in 1914. Such munitions were far less effective when used against trenches and other field works. Nevertheless Britain alone produced about a hundred million shrapnel shells during the war, most of them of the 18-pdr type.*

attack at Poelcappelle some advance was made under cover of rain, but machine guns firing from pillboxes and a barrage that moved faster than troops could wade through mud and flooded trenches reduced the tempo to a crawl. In places enemy nests were missed or bypassed and continued to harass the attackers from behind. Counterattacks now clawed back some of the ground, and both sides were left exhausted and depleted with the Germans suffering badly from 'indescribably heavy' bombardment. Gains were modest but arguably in recent days the defenders had suffered as much, or more, than the attackers.

As yet however the phase of the offensive later officially dubbed the First Battle of Passchendaele had not yet begun. This opened on 12 October with wet, cold, and exhausted troops, poorly supported, as it was

Bayernwald Trenches Opposite and Bottom left: *The Bayernwald trenches are arguably one of the most accurate reconstructions of trenches in their original locations to be found anywhere on the Western Front. The defences were so named after their Bavarian garrison, which at one point included Adolf Hitler. This part of the front was captured by British 19th (Western) Division on the first day of the battle of Messines. The site was originally unearthed by a local schoolteacher in 1971, but after his death fell into disrepair until conserved and reopened in 2004. Notice the wattle revetting, one typical method of German construction.*

Left: *Detail of one of the Bayernwald bunkers, giving a good idea of how most concrete works were originally concealed, flush with, or below ground level, and with easy access to a trench or shell holes. This bunker is of blockwork construction and surprisingly shallow internally, even after re-excavation, having insufficient space to stand upright. The Bayernwald complex comprises about 1,000ft (300m) of trenches, four bunkers and two mine shafts.*

DE TOEVALLEN VAN DEN OORLOG VEEN GEREND EN BEWAREN HUNNE

becoming increasingly difficult to shift guns and heavy supplies across the sheet of mud. The extreme conditions also served to limit the effectiveness of bombardment as shells frequently plopped deep into the ground before either exploding and blasting out a massive plume of soup-like soil, or failing to detonate. About 13,000 men Allied troops were killed or injured on the first day, many of them Australian or British, but about a quarter New Zealanders, of whom almost 900 were killed.

From the ever-present mud there was no relief. Bombardier J.W. Palmer of 26th Brigade, RA, recalled:

'It was mud, mud everywhere: mud in the trenches, mud in front of the trenches, mud behind the trenches. Every shell hole was a sea of filthy oozing mud. I suppose there is a limit to everything but the mud of Passchendaele—to see men sinking into the slime, dying in the slime—I think it absolutely finished me off. I "knew" for three months before I was wounded. I was going to get it... I thought I was going to get killed.'

Amazingly the humour of Tommy still broke through, at least amongst those that survived. One joke that circulated that autumn in Flanders, and has been found in several variants, both British and Australian, concerned a man, only his head visible, who was pulled from the mud, only to exclaim, 'Wait! Don't forget my horse...'

Though there was a pause in hope the weather would improve, and the Canadians now relieved the II Anzac Corps, the opening of Petain's attack far to the south on the Chemin des Dames, signalled an opportune moment for the second attempt on Passchendaele to begin. As so often was the case the Canadians advanced and took their objectives on 26 October, only to be hammered back by counterattack. Fighting continued again, before there was another week-long pause. A brief break in the weather finally allowed the Canadians to go forward once more, and in a final spasm from 6 to 10 November the last objectives, including the now unrecognisable ruins of Passchendaele were taken. So flattened was the village that often airmen had a better idea of where the troops were standing than those on the ground, for the outline of the foundations of the church at the centre of the village was virtually the only landmark that kept its original shape. Each side had now sustained over 200,000 casualties. These were losses that the Germans could ill afford: conversely dreams of turning the front or liberating the coast of Belgium would remain just that for almost another year.

Opposite: *The memorial to the missing designed by Sir Herbert Baker, with sculptures by John Armitage and Ferdinand Blundstone, forms the back wall of Tyne Cot. There are over 34,000 names inscribed here, the cemetery itself being the actual resting place of just under 12,000. The names of New Zealand missing are recorded within the central apse of the main wall.*

Below left: *German prisoners held by British Tommies at Pilckem Ridge, early in the battle. The cuff title worn by the standing figure suggests that the captives are Hanoverians.*

Below right: *A stretcher party makes its way across a sodden featureless landscape at Passchendaele. Recovery of casualties frequently required teams of four or more, and temporary 'corduroy' tracks of wooden logs were laid across the mire were sometimes used for the movement of men and supplies.*

Tyne Cot

The land for the cemetery was given to the United Kingdom by King Albert I of Belgium to recognise the role of Britain and its empire in the defence and liberation of Belgium. The largest Commonwealth cemetery in the world, the Cross of Sacrifice **(Below left)** *at Tyne Cot is unusual in that it is built over a German bunker, captured in October 1917— an arrangement suggested by King George V when he visited in 1922. In a stylistic nod to this the stone facing the front of the base of the cross has been sculpted to represent the blockwork of a fortification. The aperture left in its construction reveals part of the German bunker* **(Below)**. *The inscription reads, 'This was the Tyne Cot blockhouse captured by 3rd Australian Division, 4th October 1917'. The bunker served as a dressing station, and some of those who died of wounds are buried nearby.*

Right: *Tyne Cot in winter, looking north toward the Cross of Sacrifice with the memorial to the missing in the distance. In the years running up to the centenary much work has been carried out on re-engraving names on the wall, and a number of gravestones have been replaced.*

Left: *Another winter view. Perhaps surprisingly, 8,000 of the 12,000 dead are not named, so it appears likely that some mentioned on the memorial to the missing are present within the cemetery leading to double counting. Three VC winners have named graves: two Australians killed on 12 October 1917 at the battle of Broodseinde—Capt Clarence Smith Jeffries and Sgt Lewis McGee of 40th (Tasmanian) Battalion who died during repeated attacks on German bunkers—and Canadian James P. Robertson who fell on 6 November. Robertson attacked an MG post despatching four of the crew before turning the gun on the enemy. He then carried the weapon forward with his platoon, returning fire on enemy snipers, before finally being killed rescuing two men.*

Menin Gate

*The Menin Gate was designed by Sir Reginald Blomfield with sculpture by William Reid Dick, the monument was unveiled by Lord Plumer in July 1927. It serves as one of four British Empire memorials to the missing (the other three are at Thiepval, Tyne Cot and Ploegsteert). When not closed for ceremony, traffic and pedestrians flow over the cobbles, as did the troops of 1914–18 when there was only a bridge and opening in the city wall , before the gate and its vault, skylights and, of course, the names on the the of the fallen. This photo (**Opposite**) shows the panel relating to the Buffs, or East Kents. In total there are more than 54,000 names whose resting place is unknown.*

*The Last Post ceremony, (as **Below left** in September 2013), the traditional final salute to the fallen, has been played nightly at the monument by buglers of the local volunteer fire brigade since 1928, with few interruptions—most notably the German occupation of 1940–44. Over the years new instruments have been presented on a number of occasions, as for example by the Blackpool and Fleetwood 'Old Contemptibles'. If anything the ceremony is becoming more popular, often including readings, the participation of bands or associations and veterans of other wars.*

Messines

Left: *What is now known as the Pool of Peace, Spanbroekmolen. This crater was created by one of the mines blown at the opening of the battle in June 1917. Dug between January and summer 1916, it lay dormant for almost a year before detonation when 91,000lb (41,275kg) of ammonal blew a crater c.250ft (76m) in diameter. The crater was purchased by Toc H in 1929, at Tubby Clayton's suggestion. The remains of a German bunker are visible at the edge of the pool.*

Below: *Caterpillar Crater, on the other side of the railway from Hill 60, was also formed by a mine at the opening of the battle, although mine warfare had been in progress on and around Hill 60 since late 1914. No fewer than five mines were blown nearby in April 1915.*

Bottom: *Hill 60 was captured by the 11th West Yorkshires during the battle. The bottom part of this unusual concrete bunker is German, later modified by the Australians. The hill was granted to Britain after the war and was soon the site of several memorials. More recently the work of Australian tunnellers has been dramatised in the film* Beneath Hill 60.

Chapter 4
French Flanders and Artois

Previous page: *Barbed wire, Notre Dame de Lorette. see also pp102–105.*

Opposite: *The belfry, Arras, by night. The medieval town was badly damaged and extensively rebuilt: the two large central squares, the Grande Place and the Place des Héros, have been restored to essentially their prewar appearance.*

Below: *The French Flanders and Artois area showing major towns and roads with the front line as at tghe time of the battle of Arras in April 1917.*

The part of the Western Front between the Belgian border and the Somme, in the French regions of Nord and Artois, may not be as famous as other sectors. Nevertheless, few are as interesting or as of much significance, particularly if one happens to be Canadian, French, German or, indeed, British. Though parts of the landscape resemble Belgian Flanders there are significant coal deposits, and hills high enough to form not only tactical features, but to dominate the surrounding landscape. Around Loos some of these were, in fact, man-made spoil heaps, but to the south are other more important vantage points, not least the commanding features of Vimy Ridge.

For virtually all of the period 1915 to 1917 the story of Artois was that of the Germans standing on the defensive whilst the Allies strove to push the invader out. In the first phases it was the French who were dominant partner, the British attacking dutifully in support. These struggles encompassed: the First Battle of Artois from 27 September to 10 October 1914, during the so-called Race to the Sea; the Second Battle of Artois, during which the French attacked towards Vimy in May 1915; and the Third Battle of Artois, also known as the Artois-Loos offensive. Later it was the British who made the running, particularly during the Battle of Arras from 9 April to 16 May 1917. Yet at Vimy it was the Canadians who finally wrested the ridge from German grasp and, in what can only be described as a parallel to the less successful Anzac effort at Gallipoli, made a mark on world history that is remembered to this day as a coming of age for Canada. Not for nothing does the Vimy monument adorn the Canadian $20 note. Perhaps surprisingly the area is also home to the largest German war cemetery in France, as well as the largest French military cemetery. This last is at Ablain-Saint-Nazaire, though commonly known as Notre Dame de Lorette, on a humpbacked ridge that overlooks the Douai plain and also offers views toward nearby Vimy. With

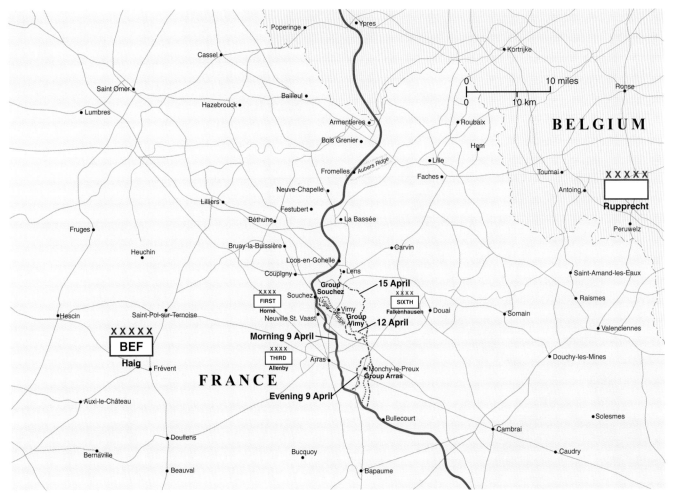

Below: *German photograph showing the aftermath of 'the attack of the English near Neuve Chappelle, 25 September, 1915'. The major attack of this date was the opening of the battle of Loos, actually some miles to the south. Some of the dead are still wearing their 'gas helmets', mute testimony to the fact that this was the first British deployment of poison gas, some of which blew back across the attacking troops. British failure was generally attributed to lack of artillery ammunition and inability to reinforce the advance.*

Bottom: *'At the battle near Neuve Chapelle: badly wounded English in the German front line', March 1915.*

a population of the dead exceeding 40,000, this dwarfs the admittedly more attractive Tyne Cot by a factor of more than three to one. The hill on which the lantern tower now sits saw fighting on and off for about a year in 1914–1915.

For the British the line southward from the Western fringes of Lille sounds like a catalogue of disappointment: Fromelles, Aubers, Neuve-Chapelle, Festubert, La Bassee and Loos. This region saw the steady expansion of British commitment, an accumulation of painfully gained experience and the downfall of Sir John French. The first commander of the BEF was no fool but had the extremely uncomfortable early experience of being told by Lord Kitchener that his main function was to hang on until the army could be expanded, and in the meantime conform to the offensive plans of his French allies, whilst not sacrificing his own forces. He was thus left at the mercy of misfortune. At the same time it has to be admitted that Sir John was not really of a temperamental disposition to command vast citizen armies, nor a natural self-publicist. Loos would be his final failure, being replaced in December 1915 by Sir Douglas Haig.

In March 1915 the British attacked at Neuve Chapelle, with British IV Corps on the left and the Indian Corps on the right. A brisk bombardment hit the enemy front line, then shifted to the village and reserve positions before the infantry went forward. After initial success with the capture of the village, the advance ground to a halt. Heavy losses included seven British battalion commanders killed or died of wounds.

Marshal Joffe issued new plans for Tenth French Army and British First Army on 6 April, in which operations on this front would form part of a three-pronged general offensive, the other attacks being launched from Verdun and Nancy in the east and from Reims. The French objective of May 1915 was the seizure of the heights at Vimy, with the main attack coming between Carency and Roclincourt. A flanking attack would take Notre Dame de Lorette, with the British advancing at Aubers. Mist and rain delayed the opening of the assault until 9 May. Methodical artillery bombardment prepared the way, but the British in particular were already short of ammunition, a deficiency that soon became the full-blown "shell scandal". Nevertheless, first reports from the French were encouraging, with General Petain managing to advance about two miles. Part of La Targette was taken, as was Souchez, before the French were

Zu den Kämpfen bei Neuve Chapelle
Schwer verwundete Engländer in der vordersten deutschen Stellung.

Once enjoying the splendid name Moggs Hole Cemetery, this small British burial ground is now known as Neuve Chappelle Cemetery, as it lies at the edge of the village and was commenced at the time of the battle.

Above: *The view down the main road from Dud Corner. Though the spoil heaps grow, and new buildings appear, the landscape maintains a little of the old industrial character of 1915.*

repelled by Bavarian Jaegers. Fighting continued for a further two weeks, but Vimy Ridge remained in German hands at the end of the struggle. At Aubers the smaller British contribution achieved even less, with a very modest initial gain snuffed out by the evening of 9 May.

Yet Foch remained fixed on the objective of Vimy, and attacked again in late May, again co-ordinating with the actions of the British. Following a 400-gun bombardment commencing on 13 May, the British attacked at Festubert two days later, in what was effectively a second instalment of the action at Aubers Ridge. Sadly the bombardment was so relatively feeble that initially the Germans did not even recognise it for what it was. In places the British broke into the enemy line, but German artillery now opened up, so that as the commander of one German battalion put it 'the earth heaved'. Little further progress was made the next day as German reinforcements were rushed in, and frantic attempts were made to repair damaged defences. Losses were far from one-sided as repeated orders were issued to oust the British from what they had managed to occupy. General Foch later blamed his allies for failure in Artois: Crown Prince Rupprecht claimed that around Arras German armies had succeeded in erecting an 'iron wall' impervious to the enemy.

The Festubert sector had a particular reputation for unpleasantness, being so boggy that at its worst it became a series of islands rather than solid ground. Coming upon the carnage of Festubert and Aubers Ridge after the actions Edmund Blunden viewed it with the detached interest of an antiquarian:

'Such as it was, the Old British Line at Festubert had the appearance great age and perpetuity; its weather-beaten sandbag wall was already venerable. It shared the past with the defences of Troy. The skulls

which spades disturbed about it were in a manner coeval with those of the most distant wars; there is an obstinate remoteness about a skull. And, as for the future, one of the first hints that came home to me was implied in a machine gun emplacement stubbornly built in brick and cement, as one might build a house... My trench education advanced, and I learned of sentry groups and trench stores, dispositions and defence schemes. I attached requisite importance to the Vermorel Sprayers for counteracting gas – simple machines such as were used in Kent to wash cherry trees with insect killer – and the clearance of match sticks illegally thrown into gutters under the duckboards...'

The old German line, attacked and passed by the British during the battle of Aubers Ridge, Blunden found, 'silent and formidable, a broad gully, like a rough sunk lane rather than a firing trench.' The whole region of Festubert 'being marshy, and undrainable, smelt ill enough, but this trench was peculiar in that way. I cared little to stop in the soft drying mud at the bottom of it; I saw old uniforms, and a great may bones, broken like bird cages. One uniform identified a German officer; the skeleton seemed less coherent than most, and an unexploded shell lay on the edge of the fragments.'

There were minor actions during the summer, but it was in September 1915 Anglo-French forces resumed the offensive at the Third Battle of Artois, timed to coincide with an attack in the Champagne. It was reasoned that if Entente forces could penetrate the German front sufficiently, vital rail nodes could be taken, thus forcing enemy retreat. French guns began bombardment on 21 September, before their main assault. On 25 September the British attacked at Loos, a small town dominated by slag heaps and the double iron towers of the pit-winding gear dubbed

Above: *Winter view over Dud Corner Cemetery, Loos, from the viewing platform. There were only five burials here at the end of hostilities, but it was enlarged by bringing together the dead from several other sites. Many were killed at the 1915 Battle of Loos. The name of the cemetery is said to derive from the number of 'dud' shells found here. The memorial to the missing which occupies the back and side of the plot commemorates more than 20,000 men.*

Opposite, above: *Australian wreath, Pheasant Wood. The new Pheasant Wood cemetery, designed by Barry Edwards, adopts many of the forms and motifs in use in the 1920s and 1930s but also incorporates features intended to assist access for the disabled.*

Opposite, below left: *Between Arras and Ypres: 'Hey mate, have you got a moment? Then hold in check for a sec Kitchener's three million army'.*

Opposite, below right: *The grave of Lt Berrol Lazar Mendelsohn, 55th Battalion, Australian Infantry, at Pheasant Wood. Mendelsohn was Jewish, as is denoted by the Star of David, and visitors have placed stones upon the grave in keeping with tradition. Jewish troops fought on both sides and Jewish symbolism also appears on French, US and German grave markers.*

Below: *German soldiers filling one of the mass graves at Fromelles. The attack at Fromelles on 19 and 20 July 1916 was intended to divert German attention from the Somme. In the wake of its bloody failure, many British and Australian casualties were buried by the enemy. However in 2009 the mass graves were excavated, and the following year the first new Commonwealth War Graves cemetery in France for half a century was dedicated at Pheasant Wood.*

Tower Bridge by the troops. For the first time the British used gas. One of the men of the 'Special Companies' tasked with the delivery of its cylinders and pipes was Ronald Purves:

'There is an awful roaring, whizzing, screaming and banging of shells. A real hell must be going on in the German trenches... Great flashes of lightning going across the sky and drizzly rain commenced, getting heavier and heavier until about eight o'clock when we had got our pipes on our shoulders... Our shoulders felt as if cut to the bone with weight of pack and pipes, we felt absolutely done up when we dropped them and passed them on... The mud was liquid and it was plastered up to our knees. We were soaked to the waist. Waterproof sheets saved our shoulders.'

When the attack came, Loos itself was overrun but gas proved a double-edged sword, and marshalling reserves quickly to the point they were needed proved impossible. The enemy chopped great holes in the assaulting battalions, as the history of German Infantry Regiment 26 reported:

'Never had machine guns such straightforward work to do, nor done it so effectively; with barrels burning hot and swimming in oil, they traversed to and fro along the enemy's ranks unceasingly; one machine gun alone fired 12,500 rounds that afternoon. The effect was devastating. The enemy could be seen literally falling in hundreds, but they continued their march in good order without interruption. The extended lines of men began to get confused by this terrific punishment, but they went doggedly on, some even reaching the wire entanglement in front of the reserve line, which their artillery had scarcely touched. Confronted by this impenetrable obstacle, the survivors turned and began to retire.'

The degree of commitment and seriousness of the losses at Loos and subsidiary attacks were underlined by the death of no fewer than three British major-generals, and three brigadiers.

Though there followed a comparative lull in Artois, 1917 would see a major Imperial effort at Arras commencing on 9 April. In this struggle 27 divisions of British, Canadian, Australian and New Zealand troops would attack on a broad front. Again the battle was co-ordinated with the French who were embarking on a major offensive under the direction of General Nivelle, about 50 miles (80km) to the south. This time, however, it was the French attack that evaporated, their new Schneider tanks coming under artillery fire, often before they could close with the German line. Many burst into flame. The enemy refused to be drawn, and main action now devolved by default to Arras. Here the Canadians stormed Vimy, and the British made gains on the Scarpe river. The opening bombardment which helped make this possible was both longer and heavier than that used on the Somme, with 2.7 million shells falling on the enemy. A short, but even more concentrated, 'hurricane' bombardment prefaced the actual infantry attack. The Germans were hard-pressed, pushed back, but, making use of more elastic defence, were not broken. Initial success again turned to attritional struggle, but the battle was ended on 16 May, thus avoiding the worst of the horrors that resulted from the much longer grinding that had already occurred at Verdun and the Somme—and was yet to happen at Third Ypres. Despite significant loss to both sides Arras has been described, not inaccurately, as a tactical victory for the Allies, but at best it was an indecisive one.

Zwischen Arras und Ypern.

„Du Kamerad, hast du 'n bischen Zeit? Dann halt doch mal für
mich 'n Augenblick Kitcheners Dreimillionen-Armee in Schach!"

G. Mühlen-
Schulte

LIEUTENANT
B. L. MENDELSOHN
55TH BN. AUSTRALIAN INF.
20TH JULY 1916 AGE 25

GREATLY LOVED SON OF
SAM AND ABIGAIL
BELOVED BROTHER OF ZILLAH
ARTHUR EVE FELIX OSCAR

Right: *Neuville St Vaast at dusk. This vast field of crosses— almost 45,000 burials—is the largest German war cemetery in France. In 1919 it was decided that it should become a 'concentration cemetery' for the German dead north and east of Arras, hence its enormous size.*

Below: *One unusual memorial at Neuville St Vaast is the monument to the 'fallen comrades' of Hanoverian Infantry Regiment Nr 164, transferred here after the war.*

Notre Dame de Lorette

The largest French military cemetery is situated northwest of Arras, the scene of the three great battles of Artois. The foundation stone of the great lantern tower (**Right**) was laid in 1921. The 160ft (52m) tower, designed by Louis-Marie Cordonnier, was not an easy build due to the poor ground conditions of the battlefield. Massive foundations and reinforced concrete were the solutions. The graves on the 'hill of the dead' are 500ft (165m) above sea level, giving views to Lille and Hazebrouck on a clear day. The site, occupying nearly 13 hectares, was designated in 1928, at which time the crosses were still of wood. As of 1933 cement crosses replaced them. Renovations and a new 'International' memorial, costing an estimated 6.5 million euros, are planned for 2014. There are 20,000 graves; the remains of 22,000 unknown soldiers were placed in eight ossuaries.

The chapel (**Above**) of the same name was destroyed; the replacement basilica replete with war memorials and incorporating salvaged stone from Bethune and Lille, was dedicated in 1927. Six of the windows were donated by the Commonwealth (then Imperial) Wargaraves Commission.

There is also a museum as exemplified by the tableau depicting French signallers inside a log bunker c.1915 (**Left**). Outside the museum are various artillery pieces including this impressive Model 1917 short 155m gun (**Top**) and this armoured sentry post (**Above left**).

Notre Dame de Lorette
The trenches at Notre Dame de Lorette before recent conservation efforts were overgrown and beginning to look like natural watercourses. Vegetation breaks up trench walls, but conversely tends to stabilize slopes. It took a great deal of work to restore and conserve them.

Vimy

Eight western front sites were provided to Canada for major memorials in 1920, five in France and three in Belgium. At Vimy an additional 250 acres on the ridge were granted in 1922. Taken together the Vimy and Beaumont Hamel memorial parks represent a significant proportion of the publicly accessible preserved battlefield sites.

The trenches were consolidated in the 1920s **(Above right)**. *Spoil heaps suggest how the trenches were dug out to an approximation of their original depth, with the earth being retained behind the cement sandbag walls.*

Here, **(Right)** *a sentry post in the German front line of the preserved Vimy trenches. In places the distance between the lines is frighteningly short: about as far as a grenade can be thrown.*

A German mortar pit at Vimy **(Below right)**. *Over a century soil creep has become very evident. Here the influx of earth has buried the concrete duckboard, and the baseplate of the mortar. Extra courses of sandbags have been added to the embrasure in an effort to stem the flow.*

The alcoves that would once have contained munitions have been replicated between the concrete sandbags of the preserved trenches **(Opposite)**. *Also apparent in this view are concrete duckboards, not terribly authentic, but much more durable than the originals. The woods in the background lie within the park, and have grown since 1918, but are still signposted as potentially dangerous.*

Vimy

Right: *A French 58mm trench mortar in the Vimy memorial park. Introduced in 1915 and firing a large finned projectile, this weapon was nicknamed the crapouillot (little toad). It soon became the standard medium mortar.*

Centre right: *For much of the year student guides employed by the Canadian department of veterans affairs provide free guided tours.*

Far right: *Inside the interpretive centre at Vimy: displays include film, a plan for orientation in the park and reproduction trench periscopes.*

Right: *Another view of the preserved Vimy trenches.*

Opposite: *The monolithic Canadian memorial at Vimy was designed by Walter Seymour Allward. Unveiled on 26 July 1936 by King Edward VIII, special passports were granted to Canadian veterans to travel to France for the ceremony. Following extensive renovations costing about Can$30 million, the memorial was rededicated by Queen Elizabeth II on 9 April 2007. Rising 95ft (30m) above the stone platform, the twin pylons of the edifice represent France and Canada. The memorial itself rests on the highest point of Hill 145, its brilliant expanse of segret limestone dominating the surrounding landscape. Embellishments to the memorial include 20 symbolic human figures representing themes such as peace and mourning. The largest single piece, Canada Bereft, was carved from a single 30-tonne block of stone. The memorial is inscribed with the names of more than 11,000 missing Canadians.*

Grange Subway

Far left: *An interwar photograph of the entrance to the Grange Subway. Nearly 2,700ft (830m) in length, the tunnel provided shelter and relatively safe movement from the rear to the front line and was just one of the many subterranean passageways constructed at Vimy by the tunnelling companies. It was used to facilitate the successful attack here in April 1917. The new concrete portal was opened in 1926.*

Left: *The entrance to Grange Subway as it appears in the early 21st century. Though the inscription and some of the relics are absent, the large shell is still in place over the door.*

Below left: *The impressive Grange Subway is not just a tunnel but also contains various byways and bunkers, some of which were constructed before the main tunnel. These house sleeping quarters, a brigade report centre, a water tank chamber and a room for a battalion CO. Men quartered here in the weeks leading up to the attack of April 1917 included personnel of Princess Patricia's Canadian Light Infantry and the Canadian Black Watch. In one place a shell has penetrated the tunnel without exploding.*

Wellington Quarry

Above right: *Inside La Carrière Wellington, Arras. The Wellington Quarry was part of the old system of ancient caves and mineworks, improved by tunnellers during the war, creating a veritable underground city in which Allied troops sheltered from bombardment. This particular complex was improved by the New Zealand Tunnelling Company from early 1916, and featured electric lighting, running water and an underground hospital. The name Wellington was taken from the capital city of New Zealand.*

Below right: *The surreal suspended walkway taking visitors through the Wellington Quarry. This amazing subterranean world was reopened as a museum in 2008. A number of artefacts remain, and in places the walls are adorned with original signs and sketches.*

CHAPTER 5
VERDUN AND THE VOSGES

Previous page and Opposite: *Officially inaugurated by French President Albert Lebrun in 1932, the great ossuary of Verdun at Douaumont contains the bones of 130,000 men, both French and German. Some of the remains can be seen through small portholes on the exterior. The tower houses a large bell, the Bourdon de la Victoire, and a light shines out over the battlefield at night.*

Below: *A German postcard showing the 'siege' of Verdun. The situation depicted is sometime between February and June 1916, with Vaux still in French hands.*

For France Verdun has a special meaning. It has come to stand as a symbol of stoicism, and of the will to protect the nation—whatever the cost. This is especially so since Verdun was not only a major and bloody battle of ultimately successful resistance, but a very French battle—not one fought with the Entente or Allies. Moreover, only by rotating troops through the Verdun front were they able to maintain enough men in good enough condition to continue the fight, and by the end of 1916 most of the army had seen some service in the sector. The battle, therefore, achieved a well-nigh universal quality: a dreadful test, that most *Poilu* of that period of the war had in common. Verdun has also been described as a watershed, after which the old enthusiasm of 1914, already battered, finally sputtered out.

During 1915 Germany had stood mainly on the defensive in the west, improving and holding what some Germans called 'God's Wall' with considerable tenacity. One defensive zone of trenches became two, then eventually three, echeloned one behind another to create a Western Front that was not just a thin defensive crust, but a belt, miles deep. There were already suspicions that a genuine war of movement and manoeuvre would be impossible until the strength and morale of enemy forces was depleted. Accordingly, having created a significant breathing space on the eastern, Russian Front, the Germans now focused their resources in the West, hoping to deal a mortal blow to their most numerous antagonist, France.

German Chief of Staff Falkenhayn believed that the French would fight hard for Verdun, and in so doing expend more of their men and energy than would the attacker. The enemy might be ground down and weakened, perhaps mortally. In the event only the first of these premises proved entirely true. For it was also the case that for many years the French had believed that they might one day be called upon to withstand attacks on Verdun, and as a result had built a complex of defences surrounding the

DieBelagerung von Verdun.

'The Tranchée des Baïonnettes is one of the great stories of Verdun. On 11 June 1916 the 137th French Infantry Regiment was preparing to advance when heavy bombardment killed many in their trench. After the action bayonets were left projecting from the earth. According to the original legend these were the weapons of the 137th left leaning on the parapet. A later explanation was that others covered over the dead, marking the graves with bayonets. The almost brutalist concrete structure over the trench was paid for by American banker George T. Rand.

city. Forts in the outer ring, clockwise from the north, included Douaumont, Vaux, Moulainville, Le Rozelier and Haudainville. Closer to the town were many more works including Belleville, Souville, Tavannes and Belrupt. Though the original fortifications were decades old, there were periodic improvements, and supplementing concrete and steel with earthworks, wire and trenches in time of war proved eminently possible. Perhaps the biggest factor hampering best use of fortifications was the fear, borne of the fate of the Belgian forts, that they were already useless. In 1915, with an ever-growing need for front-line infantry, the French high command took the decision that the forts would be held only by skeleton garrisons.

Operation Judgement began with a bombardment from more than 800 guns, growing in intensity to a final ten-hour concentration. A pause even encouraged French troops to emerge before the final deluge. The shelling, which would continue, more on than off, for months, not only tore men limb from limb by blast and jagged splinters but, when prolonged, became torment of mind and nerves. Combined with stress of battle this could lead to shell shock. As one French soldier put it:

Below: *Men of* Landwehr Infanterie Regiment Nr 40 *pose for a souvenir photo of the campaigns of 1914 and 1915. The sign on the right, underneath the little soldier figure who collects donations in his basket, reads 'we stand on the Vosges, and fight for the fatherland'.*

Bottom: *Christmas 1915 and German soldiers sing carols around a Christmas tree in a billet, 'in front of Verdun'.*

'When you hear the whistling in the distance your entire body crunches preventively together to prepare for the enormous explosions. Every new explosion is a new attack, a new fatigue, a new affliction. Even nerves of the hardest of steel, are not capable of dealing with this kind of pressure. The moment comes when the blood rushes to your head, the fever burns inside your body and the nerves, numbed with tiredness, are not capable of reacting to anything anymore. It is as if you are tied to a pole and threatened by a man with a hammer. First the hammer is swung backwards in order to hit hard, then it is swung forwards, only missing your skull by an inch, into the splintering pole. In the end you just surrender. Even the strength

Above: *The sea of graves in front of the ossuary, Verdun. There are 16,142 burials in the field. This photo was taken in 2008: in the summer of 2013 all the grave markers were replaced, as was the turf, in preparation for the centenary.*

Opposite: *Monument to the dead of French 69th Division on the Morte Homme. Unveiled in 1922 this skeletal figure is the work of sculptor Jacques Froment-Meurice, and is just one of several memorials in the vicinity. The Morte Homme vantage point on the left bank of the Meuse near Verdun was repeatedly bombarded, extensively undermined and assaulted from March 1916, finally falling in May. It was not retaken until August 1917.*

to guard yourself from splinters now fails you. There is even hardly enough strength left to pray to God...'

Three corps of German troops attacked on the afternoon of 21 February, managing an advance of about three miles by the next day. The Bois d'Haumont and the Bois des Caures both fell. By 24 February the Germans were hammering on the second line, and had reached within 6 miles (10km) of the town centre. On 25 February came a new, and partially self-inflicted, setback, as a German patrol stumbled into the ditch of Fort Douaumont and sneaked cautiously inside the poorly defended works. According to Leutnant von Brandis, 117 unprepared officers and men were captured, 'not enough to defend a huge fort like Douaumont.' The French, now commanded by General Petain, attempted to wrest back the fort the next day, but it was too late. They were overtaken by further German assaults, and now Fort Vaux was under threat.

However, having advanced only on one bank of the Meuse, the attackers found themselves under enfilade fire from artillery across the water. With progress increasingly difficult, attacks in early March focused on the Morte Homme and Hill 304 with the objective of removing enemy observers and driving the French away from the positions interfering with the advance on Verdun. At the same time fresh efforts were also made further east, against Fort Vaux. French reinforcements were pouring into the City, and whereas the Germans had started with at least a two to one advantage, this gradually slipped away to a rough parity. As French artillery strength improved, yet greater bombardments were traded and French machine guns took down increasing numbers of the enemy, despite the fact that the Germans now bobbed from shell hole to shell hole. The German Crown Prince now 'doubted more and more every day that the French, who used a quick-relief system, should suffer more

ILS N'ONT PAS PASSÉ

AUX MORTS DE LA 69ᵉᵐᵉ DIVISION

Fort Vaux
Opposite, above: *One of Fort Vaux's 75mm guns, still in place inside a casemate.*

Opposite, below: *Corridor to the outside world: Fort Vaux. By early June 1916 the German attackers had succeeded in entering the fort through its ditch: battles with flamethrowers and grenades ensued.*

Below: *Plaque commemorating the pigeon, Fort Vaux. With the fort cut off and supplies failing, Commandant Raynal was reduced to communicating by carrier pigeon. The last bird delivered Raynal's final message, then expired: the pigeon was later decorated for its efforts. Vaux was forced to surrender on 7 June 1916, the German Crown Prince allowing Raynal to retain his sword as a mark of respect for his gallantry. The fort remained in German hands until November.*

losses than we did.' Nevertheless, by a stupendous uphill struggle, both the Morte Homme and Hill 304 were taken by late May.

In the first days of June the struggle for Vaux reached its climax. The Germans occupied the roof, deployed machine guns to prevent reinforcement, then attempted to take the fort in close-quarter battle. As Capt Gagneur of 101st French Infantry Regiment recalled:

'The Germans work us over with flamethrowers: black smoke penetrates the casemates, and the dull crack of hand grenades comes closer and closer. We cannot breathe, and we are as black as Moors. To get air we must open a port. Very cautiously and gradually we move away the sandbags... We have the great luck that there are no Germans in the trench. Some jump out to get air. But we must get back in— the order of the Commander, "block all exits"... a few people start to panic, but Lt Bazy, located at the barricade, jumps behind the machine gun and, infuriated, pours fire on the advancing Germans. Hand grenades are then thrown bravely over the barrier.'

Eventually, however, the heroic resistance of Fort Vaux was quenched on 7 June following a hand-to-hand battle in the galleries.

The fight for Thiaumont still raged. As the French Capt Delvert observed of the scene at his position, 'In our trenches, it is a tragedy; everywhere stones are spotted with red drops. In the saps stiff corpses are lying in their tent sheets which are covered with blood; there are heaps of unnameable remains everywhere.'

New waves of German assaults began on 21 June, and these were answered by French counterattacks. The result was violent equilibrium, with the Germans making little progress. Now Fort Souville was stoutly defended as enemy attackers climbed across its roof engaging in grenade duels, but the Germans did reach and take Fleury, where, but for a few stumps of wall, the village had ceased to exist. By early July it became increasingly apparent that time had run out. With the British attacking with an almost reckless abandon on the Somme, and the French defenders of Verdun trading life for life, the only option was to call a halt. On 12 July the German Crown Prince was forced to concede that for now his forces would adopt a 'strictly defensive position'. Despite this order there was still heavy, if indecisive, fighting around Fleury in August, and in September the Germans were pushed back from Souville. After a lull it was the French who went onto the offensive. By late October Douaumont was back in their hands, but it would be 1917 before the Morte Homme and Hill 304 were reclaimed.

Verdun, which combined bombardment, repeated infantry attacks, siege warfare, flame and gas in confined spaces created new levels of devastation. As a French soldier at the Morte Homme towards the end of the battle reported:

'There is not, in fact, one square metre of soil intact. Everywhere the artillery has dug craters, some of which are 6m [20ft] deep, 8m [26ft] wide, or even more. All around lumps of earth and stones have fallen back like an avalanche, crushing everything where it fell. The terrain is completely destroyed—the wheat fields are gone, though we still see the soil in our lines... We entered the *Kronprinz* tunnel, and for 2km [1.25 miles] were forced to endure a nauseating stench... Two staircases, one up, one down a metre [c. 3ft] wide. The corridor is flooded because a water pipe was punctured by our shells... We met the men of a medical unit yesterday who had taken three crazy Hun prisoners there. They

Top: *German soldiers well concealed in a front-line trench in the Vosges, rifles aimed through loopholes, March 1915.*

Above: *A contemporary German postcard* In den Vogesen *(in the Vosges) showing a machine gun and riflemen at work. Though battlefield conditions were very different and warfare was often at a lower intensity than on the Flanders plain or at Verdun, the Vosges occupied a major portion of the front and saw long periods of stasis.*

had spent five days immured with corpses before being removed from their holes by rope. The doctor had pity on them, keeping them in the infirmary for 48 hours before sending them back.'

The 'red zone' of total destruction after the war, comprised overlapping shell craters, mud, lumps of concrete and pieces of twisted metal and humanity covering about 39 square miles (100sq km).

For Britons and North Americans it is often something of a surprise to discover that Verdun stands, even as the crow flies, much more than 100 miles (160km) from Switzerland. Following the Western Front, via St Mihiel, and around to the east of Nancy, which never fell to the Germans, to the border village of Pfetterhouse and the Three Powers Boundary Stone makes this distance greater still. (The *Borne des Trois Puissances*, or Three Powers Boundary Stone, is in Pfetterhouse, an Alsatian village. Until 1919, it was the point where the borders of France, Germany and Switzerland met.) Though the duration and intensity of combat in the southernmost part of the front cannot readily be compared with Verdun or the Somme, there were still lines of trenches, bombardments and indeed battles. The Rhine plain of Alsace in particular saw action in 1914 when attempts were made to seize this territory, which was French before 1871. Mulhouse was twice occupied before German Seventh Army consolidated their hold. In September 1914, during the battle of Grand Couronné, the French army succeeded in blocking the advance of Prince Rupprecht. In parallel to the battle of the Marne and the march on Paris, the Germans were thus prevented from reaching Nancy. Between St Die and Mulhouse the Western Front climbs into the Vosges mountains whose peaks rise 4,500ft (1,400m) above sea level. In such conditions a very different sort of local war was fought, sometimes on skis, and in which terrain it was possible, however briefly, for units to create semi-fluid micro-fronts as one side held a peak and the other attempted to manoeuvre around it or moved unseen along valleys. Perhaps unsurprisingly however there would never be a dramatic breakthrough in the mountains.

Voie Sacrée

Main photo: *The Monument Commemoratif du Train on the Voie Sacrée, the road that was Verdun's wartime lifeline back to Bar-le-duc. In 2006 the route was renumbered RD1916 to commemorate this vital role. It has been calculated that at the height of the battle a truck passed this way every 14 seconds. Whole battalions were required to maintain the road.*

Inset, below: *Detail of the Voie Sacrée monument showing French gunners handling shells. Unveiled in 1967 the monument was created by architects G. Schmitt and F. Barrois, with sculpture by J.A. Barrois.*

Verdun

Above left: *L'ouvrage de Thiaumont was one of the small fortlets covering gaps between the major works of the Verdun defences. Commenced in 1887, it was extensively modernised by 1905. In 1916 it was protected by wire and mounted two machine guns. Heavily shelled it fell to the Germans on 23 June, and thereafter was taken and retaken in counterattacks. Today it is recognisable only as humps and pieces of twisted metal amongst a field of shell holes.*

Above: *Verdun, set on the Meuse and with a network of canals, as it appears today. The town mounts an annual sound and light show 'based around a scenic representation of the battle'. This is billed as having 250 actors, 900 costumes and 1,000 projectors.*

Below left: *Memorial of Le Soldat du Droit to Lt Andre Thome, killed at Verdun, March 1916. Thome was a member of the French parliament and volunteered to fight.*

Above right: *A de Bange-type 155mm French heavy artillery piece in front of the Memorial Museum, Fleury, Verdun. This excellent museum, which stands on the site of a railway station destroyed in the battle, was one of the many facilities improved in 2013 ahead of the centenary. Fleury village, high watermark of the German offensive, captured and recaptured many times, has been left abandoned: 'a village that died for France'.*

Right: *London Trench winds its way through the woodland of Verdun. During the battle vegetation was blown from large areas of the landscape. After the war woods were allowed to cover large tracts of the shelled ground of what was once dubbed the 'capital of the war', and more recently, the 'town of world peace'.*

Fort Douaumont

Far left: *One of the armoured observation cupolas atop Fort Douaumont, Verdun. The roof was of reinforced concrete 20ft (6m) thick, and at the height of the battle it was struck many hundreds of times by shells of all calibres.*

Left: *Inside Fort Douaumont's 155mm armoured gun turret. Built between 1907 and 1909 the turret was capable of turning and retracting by means of a system of hand-cranked geared wheels.*

Bottom left: *French memorial, Fort Douaumont, Verdun. Items such as gun barrels, loophole plates and shells of different sizes decorate the shrine. The 'Lazarett' sign is from a dressing station during the German occupation of the fort.*

Above right: *A Nahkampfshikane in the Douaumont tunnels. These obstructions with loopholes gave cover during close-quarter battle, preventing attackers from shooting straight along corridors. In some of the Verdun forts there are also special loops allowing unseen defenders to drop grenades through holes.*

Right: *A dormitory in Fort Douaumont. As the biggest of the Verdun's 19 forts, Douaumont was capable of accommodating a garrison of 635. In 1914 it was actually occupied by an infantry company, plus artillerymen and engineers. However, it was soon concluded that the latest siege guns rendered the work obsolete, so as of August 1915 much of the armament and manpower was removed. This left just one 155mm and one 75mm gun and 57 reservists.*

Below right: *'To the dead comrades': the German memorial inside Douaumont. The memorial consists of a cross set against a blocked up corridor. On 8 May 1916, during the German occupation of the fort, there was a catastrophic explosion and fire attributed careless cooking, leading to detonation of the hand grenade store, and an ignition of flamethrower fuel and other munitions. There is disagreement between sources on the precise number of fatalities but these certainly numbered hundreds, a figure of 679 being widely quoted. Many were permanently entombed behind this wall in what a German language guidebook of the interwar period called 'Artillery bunkers 1 and 2'.*

Butte de Vauquois

Left: *The lantern monument to the dead on the Butte de Vauquois. Designed by Monestier Roussel, the lantern was built in 1926 by the site of the old village town hall. It remains surrounded by chevaux de frise obstacles, barbed wire and remnants of bunkers. The village was rebuilt at the foot of the ridge.*

Below left: *The landscape of craters at the Butte de Vauquois, showing tiny figures of workers clearing vegetation in advance of 2014. With the feature in German hands, mine warfare commenced early in 1915, both sides tunnelling under the hill and blowing out sections of the lines. By that autumn, mines were being detonated every few days, with 17 mines in November 1915 alone. As years passed the explosions got bigger, with charges of anything up to 22,000lb (10,000kg).*

Overleaf (page 128): *A section of German trench on the Butte de Vauquois. At times French and German lines here were only a few yards apart. Mine galleries still exist under what remains of the hill, and have been the subject of extensive exploration.*

Below: *Postcard depicting the removal of the Vauquois bell. With the church destroyed and converted into a strongpoint, the bell was dug out and taken behind German lines. Here it rang in the New Year of 1915, much to the mystification of French troops within earshot.*

Right: *Sculpture of a French grenadier on the memorial lantern of the Butte de Vauquois.*

French national monument Hartmannsweilerkopf
Right: *Interwar postcard showing the cemetery at Hartmannsweilerkopf.*

Below: *Monument to the dead of the French 152nd Infantry, the Red Devils, on the Hartmannsweilerkopf. Skirmishing on the slopes commenced in late 1914, and soon the French Chasseurs Alpine were dug in on the peak. The Germans surrounded them and captured the objective and so began a tit-for-tat battle. The 152nd were virtually destroyed here in December 1915.*

CHAPTER 6
THE SOMME, 1916

Previous page: *The imposing Thiepval memorial to the missing was designed by Sir Edwin Lutyens. Opened in 1932, it commemorates more than 72,000 dead whose graves are unknown. Thiepval village, an objective of 1 July, finally fell to British 18th Division on 26–27 September.*

Below: *The battle of the Somme started on 1 July with the detonation of the Hawthorn Redoubt mine. The final push— the battle of the Ancre—ended on 18 November after limited British successes that saw 45,000 German casualties including 7,000 prisoners.*

Opposite: *The grave plot shared by Kanonier Fritz Dies and Obergefreiter Wilhelm Holz at Sapignies German cemetery just north of Bapaume: both lost their lives early in the Somme battle.*

The distinctive topography of the Somme is much at variance with the flat and watery aspect of Flanders. For on the Somme the generous rolling terrain of farmland and small villages is based on solid chalk, a broad anticline which is an extension of the Kentish and Sussex Weald. Various thicknesses of frost-broken chalk, clay with flints, and loam overlie the virgin rock, and whilst thick caking mud occurs in wet weather, the ground is eminently suitable for tunnelling and entrenchment. Once taken early in the war, its German occupiers would prove loath to shift, quite literally rooting themselves into the soil with deep dugouts, obstacle zones, and well laid trenches. By 1916 they had begun a third line of trenches, behind two already constructed, creating a defended belt around five miles (8km) thick. The first line skirted around Curlu, Maricourt, Montauban, Fricourt, La Boiselle and Thiepval north to Hebuterne. The second fronted Maurepas, Guillemont and Grandcourt; the third, Flers, Le Sars and Achiet le Petit. Woods, such as Mametz, Delville, Bernafay and Trones relieved the scenery, but when broken down by shells created almost impenetrable tangles of branches making navigation and command of troops well nigh impossible.

The battle of the Somme, famously referred to by Capt von Hentig of the General Staff as the 'muddy grave of the German field army', was also a watershed of the war for Britain and France. For the British it would see the mass-commitment of Kitchener's New Armies who were largely recruited on the wave of popular enthusiasm that had begun in August 1914, and gradually began to peter out in 1915. It would also bring home, through huge casualties and the novel medium of film, the reality of that war to the localities of Britain. For France the Somme relieved the hideous pressure on Verdun, but also created growing uneasiness that the nation's resources were finite, and that the increasing contribution of her ally could mean that she might not ultimately be sole mistress of her own destiny. Whilst French operations in the southern part of the Somme

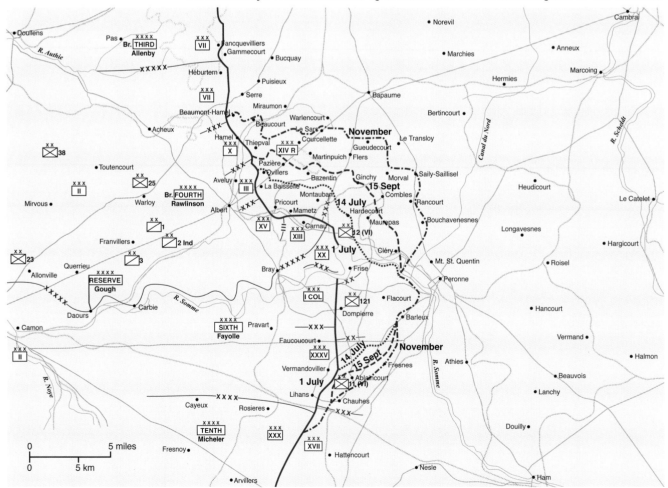

The French memorial at Longueval. Near to both Delville Wood and High Wood the village is site to both New Zealand and Scottish memorials. This one may serve as reminder that the French also fought on the Somme before the sector was occupied by British and Imperial forces.

sector were arguably more successful than those of her British partner, they were stunted by the need to keep large numbers of troops circulating through Verdun, and Marshal Ferdinand Foch faced increasing criticism over strategy and ever spiralling losses.

The decision to make a 'Big Push' on the Western Front in 1916 had its roots in late 1915 in the second inter Allied conference at Chantilly. Agreements were reached that efforts on the various fronts should be better coordinated, and that when one partner was attacked others should launch offensives. Britain and France soon concluded on a joint effort for the following summer, and with the replacement of Sir John French British planning now fell to the new Commander in Chief of the BEF, Sir Douglas Haig. The Somme, being viewed as both a promising and relatively quiet sector with space to deploy, was also selected on grounds of administrative convenience as it marked the boundary between British and French armies. Originally the French were to be senior partners, but with advent of German operations at Verdun, the French contribution was progressively scaled back. Moreover, Haig now came under pressure to bring the date for the attack on the Somme forward a month.

The final scheme saw the main initial British burden borne by Gen Sir Henry Rawlinson's Fourth Army. Crucial to the plan of attack was a massive bombardment, eventually extended to a week, followed by advance on a broad front from Serre in the north to Foucaucourt in the south. The juncture between the British and French sectors fell just north of Maricourt, and a diversionary attack was mounted at Gommecourt by Allenby's Third Army. Previous offensives were thought to have been stymied for two major reasons: failure to use enough artillery, and failure to reinforce advances in timely fashion. The Somme was planned to remove both deficiencies in spades. Artillery would blast the enemy from the creases of the earth and cut his wire, and the infantry was programmed to advance maintaining momentum by continuous reinforcement from the rear. As the artillery would clear the enemy from the front lines the infantry could go forward steadily, neither exhausting themselves prematurely nor losing their co-ordination. The real fight would start once the British were in possession of the enemy lines, with the next body of fresh troops ready to push through the first and exploit the gap created.

It would be wrong to say that no progress at all was made on 1 July, as there were advances in the south with 30th Division, for example, seizing Montauban. The French, more successful with their guns and more willing to use

Below: *Typical Commonwealth War Graves signage at Longueval on the Somme. Caterpillar Valley, on the way to Guillemont, was captured after very fierce fighting in the latter part of July 1916, but the cemetery was commenced by 39th Welsh Division in 1918. Thistle Dump at High Wood was a front-line cemetery from August 1916. London Cemetery, begun with 47 men buried in a shell hole, is third largest on the Somme, containing almost 4,000 graves, most of unidentified men. Longueval Road cemetery was begun near a dressing station.*

Above: *Inside a German machine-gun post. Artillery may have been the biggest killer of the war, but machine guns combined with barbed wire were crucial and effective in close defence.*

Opposite: *The view from Hawthorne Ridge, near the mine crater, towards Beaumont Hamel British cemetery. The village eventually fell on 13 November 1916. Some of the dead from this attack and subsequent operations were buried here in a cemetery designed by W.H. Cowlishaw.*

flexible skirmish lines to front their attacks, made gains. John Masefield would view the *Old Front Line* of the Somme as the starting place not only from which 'the biggest battle in which our people were ever engaged' commenced, but as the point of departure from which the enemy realised 'he was beaten'. This feeling that the Somme proved that the British Army had strength and stomach for a massive task, only dimly apprehended hitherto, was also iterated by many survivors. Nevertheless, the first day of the Somme was, and remains, the British Army's bloodiest day ever. Some of the objectives of 1 July remained in German hands three months later. And like many a cliché, the folk memory of long lines emerging from the ground at the blast of a whistle and walking steadily forward, only to be scythed down by machine guns contains much more than an awful grain of truth. A total of 19,240 died, with many more wounded, bringing the overall total to 57,470 casualties. Signaller Dudley Menaud-Lissenburg saw 29th Division go 'over the top':

'I watched with mixed feeling the lads mount the firestep and, when at 7.30 the barrage lifted, spring up the ladders on to the parapet— many sliding back immediately when they reached the top, killed or wounded. Cooly, it seemed, the survivors worked their way through our barbed wire in the face of fierce shell and machine gun fire, leaving many of their pals on the wire, dead. On they went up the long incline in perfect order, dropping to the ground every now and then, as though on an exercise on Salisbury Plain. The line thinned as men fell, but never faltered.'

This, however, was but the start of a battle spanning from the hopeful beginning of July to the cold and wet of a more disillusioned November, when it was concluded that weather—if nothing else—precluded a

Opposite, above right:
Newfoundlander and Inniskilling Fusilier share a grave at Y-Ravine Cemetery. Murphy hailed from Petty Harbor Newfoundland; Marsland from Liverpool. The cemetery was created in 1917 when the Beaumont Hamel battlefield was cleared.

Opposite, above left: *Looking on a hot summer's day from the remains of the German trenches towards the little Hunter's Cemetery, Beaumont Hamel. The Reverend Hunter was Chaplain to the Black Watch, one of the regiments of 51st Highland Division that finally captured Beaumont Hamel. The circular cemetery was once just a large shell hole. Now 41 identified dead are commemorated here, no fewer than 32 Black Watch: the remainder are Gordon Highlanders, one from the Royal Scots, and 21-year old Lt Gerald Sydney Smith of the Machine Gun Corps. All of them died in November 1916.*

Opposite, below: *The Accrington Pals memorial at Sheffield Memorial Park, near Serre. From trenches in the copses at the foot of a gentle slope, shallow parts of which remain visible, the Accrington, Barnsley and Sheffield Pals of 31st Division began their attack of 1 July. The Accrington Brick memorial was dedicated in 1991.*

Right: *Drummers of German Reserve Infanterie Regiment Nr 55. This unit fought with distinction on the Somme, beginning with counterattacks mounted at Gommecourt on 1 July.*

breakthrough that year. Those more than four months contained many low points. Trones Wood and Guillemont for example were undoubtedly amongst the troughs, these being attacked repeatedly, and often unimaginatively, until the unburied dead, of both sides, littered a featureless landscape of overlapping shell craters that stank in the summer sun. With gains measured in yards the attritional nature of the struggle came to feature more highly than strategic significance. Haig spoke of a 'wearing out' battle, his intelligence officers looking to an illusory breaking of German morale that might spell a beginning of the end for the war.

The Somme was indeed a trial of morale for all, whether French, German, or British. Just how bad conditions could be is well illustrated by a nightmare journey along Longueval Alley, a trench that ran from 'Hell Corner', through Bernafay Wood, around Trones to the remains of Longueval village and on to Delville Wood, made by Stanley Spencer, then a private with the Royal Fusiliers:

'Longueval Alley was in an awful state. It was a German trench and had been shelled to pieces. It was extremely wide and shallow and was soaked in gas and blood and the acrid smell of high explosive. It was full of dead men, both visible—lying about as they had been killed in the trench itself—and invisible—killed and buried with loose earth from the caved in sides of the trench—and now formed part of the floor in which everyone walked. One man had his head and shoulders blown away and the rest of his body and internal organs lay about the trench while odd hands and legs of others lay just by. Further up five men lay close together, one leaning back with wide open eyes and mouth, a jack-knife in one hand and a tin of bully beef held tightly in the other. Another man sat astride a low wall in front of a cubby hole; he was leaning forward on his arms and remained so for days, though the cubby hole was often occupied.'

On a much less obvious up side, there were certain significant facts to illuminate such gloom. The first was that the objective of relieving the pressure on Verdun was quite swiftly achieved. The campaign of Chief of Staff Falkenhayn against the city and its fortified ring had reached its zenith, and a generally defensive posture was adopted after mid-July. He himself was deposed in favour of Hindenburg at the end of August. Reserves were required in great numbers to shore up

the Somme front, a point graphically illustrated by maps of German dispositions. Between Peronne and Monchy there were barely seven divisions on the front line on 1 July: by November this had become 18, many of them severely battered and depleted, with some having suffered a double dose of both Verdun and Somme. If British tactics of 1 July had been sadly awry, and absurdly optimistic, those of the

196 PRIVATE
L. MURPHY
ROYAL NEWFOUNDLAND REGT
1ST JULY 1916
REQUIESCAT IN PACE

52 PRIVATE
MARSLAND
INNISKILLING FUS.
JULY 1916 AGE 20
NEVER FORGOTTEN
HIS LOVING MOTHER
SISTERS & BROTHERS

DEDICATED TO THE MEMORY
OF ALL MEMBERS OF THE
"ACCRINGTON PALS"
SO MANY OF WHOM FELL HERE
DURING THE ATTACK ON
SERRE 1st JULY 1916
IN THE OPENING PHASE
OF THE
BATTLE OF THE SOMME

THEIR NAME LIVETH
FOR EVERMORE

1914 — 1918
EGYPT

Right: *A British 9.45-inch heavy trench mortar team at Pigeon Wood Gommecourt, early 1917. Nicknamed the 'flying pig' this weapon was based on a similar French design. It entered British service in 1916.*

Below: *A German communication trench wends its way through an unidentified village. Even small hamlets could be made strongpoints by reinforcing cellars, emplacing machine guns and wiring. Communication trenches allowed unseen reinforcements to come in and wounded to go out.*

Opposite, above: *View from a mass grave across Fricourt German cemetery. More than 17,000 bodies are interred here, many of them in the four communal graves. The dead from many smaller cemeteries were concentrated by the French authorities from 1920. At one point the 'Red Baron', Manfred von Richtofen, was buried here, though his remains were subsequently reburied in Berlin and later Wiesbaden.*

Opposite, below: *View of the battlefield from the road by the cemetery at Ovillers. British 8th and 34th Divisions attacked around here on 1 July.*

Germans in the following weeks were also at fault, but for different reason, as counterattacks strove to regain churned slivers of France, and often seized them, at a price in blood that could but ill be afforded.

British methods did improve during the battle. Lengthy bombardments that ceased suddenly or 'lifted' onto distant targets were replaced by creeping barrages to which the infantry were instructed to cling as closely as possible. Rigid advances in broad daylight gave way to more flexibility and night and dawn action. Some attacks, like that of the 7th Bedfords at Thiepval on 27 September, were not announced by bombardment at all, being carried by surprise with 'bomb and bayonet'. New gas masks, better shell fuses and a variety of other gadgets made their appearance, but perhaps the most dramatic and important development of all came at Flers on 15 September, with the first ever appearance of the tank in battle. Interestingly, the new armoured tracked vehicle could have been called almost anything, but 'tank' was originally a cover, used to make a curious enemy believe that what was being moved up to the front was merely a type of water tank. This was not so farfetched when one realises that water was often in short supply in the trenches and that water tanks of the period were often metal, oblong, riveted constructions. From the point of view of the German infantryman first impressions were both mysterious and terrifying.

After the war, and possibly tastelessly considering that many of the survivors were still living, there would be a long running paper dispute as to whether the Allies or Germans had suffered the greater loss. We may never know precise figures, but the total number of casualties on all sides, wounded and missing as well as dead, certainly exceeded one million. One estimate is that German casualties were about 465,000; the British 420,000; and French 204,000. Despite the enormity of such bald statistics, and subsequent claims by both sides, they do not support the idea of any outright victory, German or Allied. The proportion of loss was somewhat against the British and French, though arguably rather less so than one might have expected with the Germans defending well-protected positions. Conversely, though advances were made, to pretend that they were other than trivial given the distance to Berlin, or the value of the shattered hamlets gained, would be fallacious.

Delville Wood

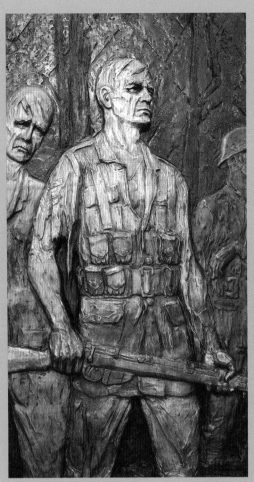

Right: *South African memorial, Delville Wood, by Sir Herbert Baker. What became known as the battle of Delville Wood lasted from 14 July to 3 September 1916. The South Africans quickly took part of the wood, but fighting or even digging amongst tree roots and fallen trees, under artillery fire, proved catastrophically costly. Repeated attempts were made before the wood was secured in the teeth of German counterattack.*

Left: *Detail of a bronze panel within the museum of the Delville memorial depicting exhausted South Africans at what they dubbed 'Devil's Wood'. Vestiges of trenches, along with stone markers, remain in the wood.*

Opposite: *The Tank Corps Memorial, Pozières. Unveiled in 1922, this memorial incorporates the names of tank actions and has four small model tanks around the obelisk. The memorial boundary is comprised of tank gun barrels linked by tank driving chains.*

Right: *The last resting place of Sgt Herbert Howley of the 11th East Lancashire Regiment—the Accrington Pals—at Queen's Cemetery, Puisieux. Howley was just one of the 584 men of the battalion killed, wounded or missing on 1 July.*

Peronne

Above left: *Peronne in ruins. Armies passed through more than once and during the battle of the Somme the town was shelled by French guns. When the Germans retreated in 1917 the town was occupied by the British. Lost again in 1918, Peronne was finally liberated, as ruins, by Australian troops.*

Below left: *The medieval gateway of Peronne. The town has been restored since 1918, and is now home to the substantial Historial de la Grande Guerre museum opened in 1992. Displays are captioned in English, French and German, and facilities include a research centre.*

Auchonvillers

Above right: *Covered trenches at Auchonvillers, just behind the British lines opposite Beaumont Hamel. Systematic excavation began here in 1997 revealing a brick-floored trench running from the cellar of a building, rebuilt in 1923, and now used as tea rooms. On the basis of archaeological evidence it is believed that the reserve company of the battalion holding the nearby front line was quartered here.*

Right: *Belgian and British tourists examine a reopened trench running up to the tea rooms at Auchonvillers, a spot known to British troops as 'Ocean Villas'. Both Edmund Blunden and John Masefield left descriptions of buildings around here, the latter mentioning that several structures of red brick remained even in 1917.*

Newfoundland Memorial Park
As might be expected, the Newfoundland Memorial Park, opened by FM Douglas Haig in 1925, focuses on the story of the Newfoundland Regiment and 1 July 1916. Nevertheless, the French fought here earlier in the war, and many British units are also commemorated. Within the park are located the 29th and 51st Highland Division memorials and three cemeteries. There is also an excellent visitor centre (Below). The park is dominated by the bronze Newfoundland Caribou monument, sculpted by Basil Gotto, which rises from atop a bunker (Left and Right). At the base of the Caribou is the memorial to the missing of Newfoundland, recording the names of over 800 lost on land and at sea. On 1 July 1916 the 29th Division advance at Beaumont Hamel was preceded by the blowing of the Hawthorne Ridge mine by ten minutes. By the time the attack came the enemy had occupied their trenches and opened fire. In the second wave the Newfoundland Regiment took the second highest loss of any battalion that day, 684 killed, wounded and missing. The original British trenches (Below right), once adorned with barbed wire and other original metal objects, have been fitted with new duckboards.

Thiepval

*Dominated by the huge Lutyens memorial, in recent years a visitor centre has been discreetly added to the site. In the clearing of the plot for the centre, archaeologists discovered German bodies, shells, remains of gas masks and large quantities of grenades—although the graves here are primarily British and French. Here (**Right**), an educational group studies a re-excavated British mortar pit in Thiepval Wood. The pit was constructed to allow high-angle fire without exposing the crew.*

Left: *A guide shows one of the re-excavated trenches in Thiepval Wood which were occupied by men of 36th (Ulster) Division before their attack on the morning of 1 July. Various items unearthed here included unexploded shells, bully beef tins, a spoon and rum jars.*

Below and Right: *Near Thiepval is the Ulster Tower, a memorial to 36th (Ulster) Division opened in 1921. The monument is close to the site of the Schwaben Redoubt and incorporates a small museum. The painting shows Ulstermen defending a trench against counter-attack.*

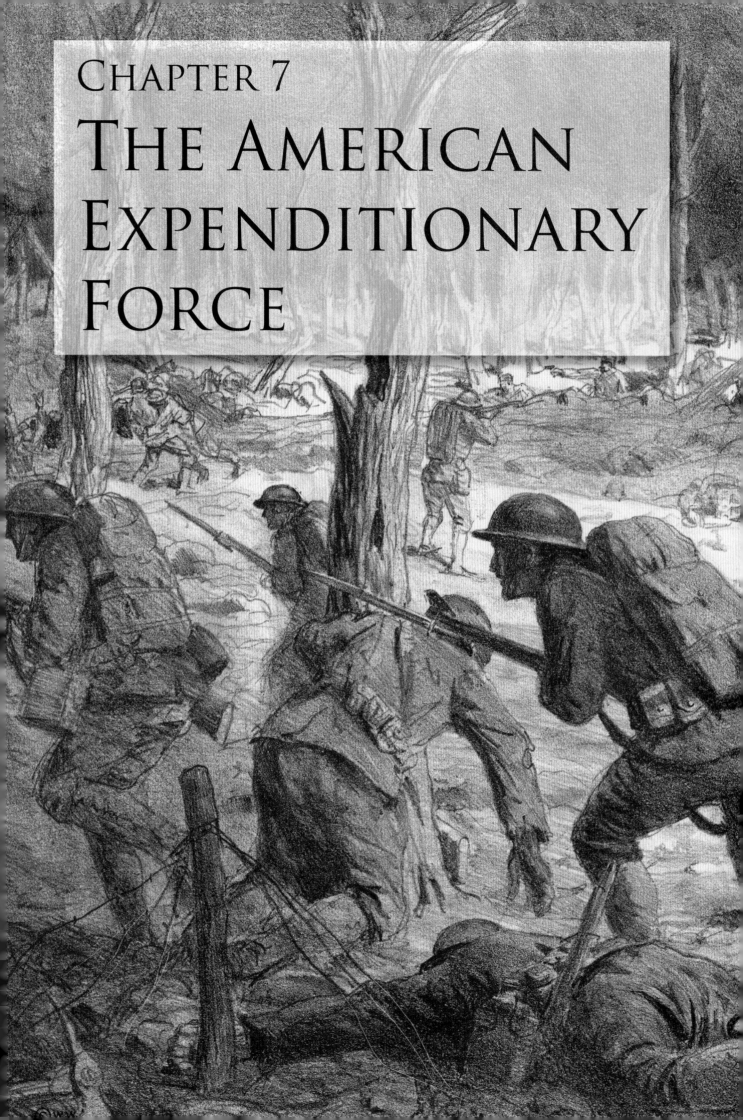

CHAPTER 7
THE AMERICAN EXPENDITIONARY FORCE

Previous page: *'An infantry attack in woods at Argonne front,' after Lucien Jonas.*

Below: *The Meuse-Argonne offensive of September–November 1917, which saw the first significant US involvement on the Western Front.*

Opposite: *Steel helmets hanging in the private Romagne 14–18 museum at Romagne-sous-Montfaucon. This collection, like many similar along the front, consists of battlefield finds; highly atmospheric but rusting. The shallow steel helmet designed by Brodie was used by both British and US forces.*

By 1917 the fact that the 'Great War' was also a 'World War' was remarkably well reflected on the Western Front. A few Austrians and others were to be seen on the German side, but in aid of the Allies came a steady and growing flow of new combatants to add to the French, British and Belgians. The troops of France and Britain's empires and dominions were amongst the first, and these included Indians, North Africans, Australians, New Zealanders, Canadians, South Africans, New Foundlanders and Senegalese. The Tsar began sending Russians in early 1916. The same year Germany declared war on Portugal, and her troops began to arrive early in 1917. Italians fought on the Western Front in small numbers in the latter part of the war. Chinese were also present, though as labourers rather than fighters. A Polish division, fighting as part of French Fourth Army, would take to the field in the west in 1918. The big question in the minds of diplomats and generals however was whether the US would join the war, and when her troops might arrive.

Arguably the policy of US neutrality first came under pressure in 1915 with the sinking of the *Lusitania*. In fact a number of Americans joined the war at an early stage with volunteers crossing the northern border to don Canadian uniform or proffering their services direct to France, notably as ambulance crew. Airmen also flew for France with a full American *Escadrille 124* taking to the air in 1916. Despite domestic resistance, pressure to enter the war continued to mount until early 1917 when German diplomatic and military blunder transformed the entire situation. With unrestricted submarine warfare about to recommence Germany offered Mexico support in recovering the southern part of the United States, lost during the Mexican-American War. News of this astonishing proposal surfaced when the Zimmerman telegram—from Arthur Zimmermann, the German Foreign Secretary, to the German ambassador in Mexico, Heinrich von Eckardt, was revealed:

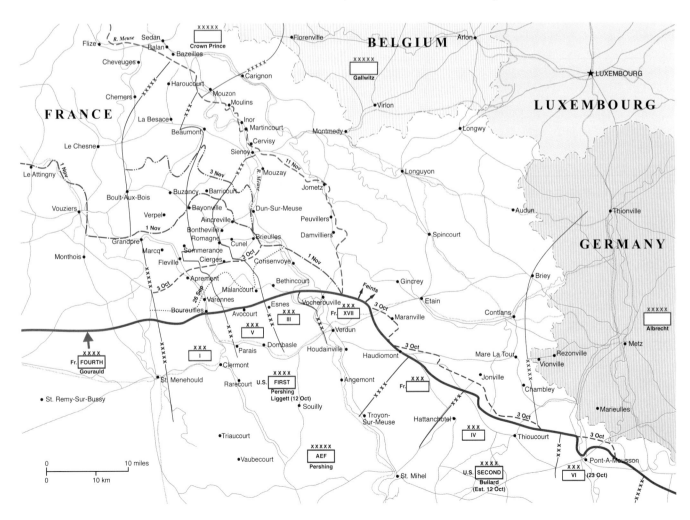

Ruined bridge at St Mihiel. The attack at St Mihiel in September 1918 was part of a bigger attempt by the US Army to break through and capture the town of Metz. Half a million Americans were supported by four divisions of French troops. Despite wind, rain and mud assaulting the St Mihiel salient on two fronts proved successful against inferior German forces who had already begun withdrawal against the possibility of becoming surrounded. There were about 7,000 casualties on either side, and a greater number of Germans captured, the subsequent advance towards Metz being abandoned in favour of supporting the offensive in the Meuse-Argonne sector.

'We intend to begin on the first of February unrestricted submarine warfare. We shall endeavor in spite of this to keep the United States of America neutral. In the event of this not succeeding, we make Mexico a proposal of alliance on the following basis: make war together, make peace together, generous financial support and an understanding on our part that Mexico is to reconquer the lost territory in Texas, New Mexico, and Arizona. The settlement in detail is left to you. You will inform the President of the above most secretly as soon as the outbreak of war with the United States of America is certain and add the suggestion that he should, on his own initiative, invite Japan to immediate adherence and at the same time mediate between Japan and ourselves. Please call the President's attention to the fact that the ruthless employment of our submarines now offers the prospect of compelling England in a few months to make peace.'
Signed, ZIMMERMANN

With US ships being sunk, President Wilson went to Congress: the declaration of war followed on 6 April 1917. Technically, the US then became an associated power in the struggle against Germany. In May Maj-Gen John 'Black Jack' Pershing (1860–1948) was put in command of the American Expeditionary Force (AEF).

However, the US Army was small, far away, and lacked experience of large-scale modern European war. The first troops departed quickly, but as of June 1917 only 14,000 'Doughboys' arrived in France, and it was October before 1st US Division reached the trenches near Nancy. As a result US troops first saw action as units fighting within bigger French and British sectors, and often with equipment supplied or designed by them. If Americans had any illusions about war on the Western Front, they were quickly punctured, as Lt K.E. Walser, 101st Field Artillery, wrote home to his family in February 1918:

'I laughed till I cried when you said you were going to send me *The Glory of the Trenches*, for I was standing in the stickiest mud that ever existed, watching a bombardment to our left and reading your letter at the same time. Believe me, the ground was a mass of shell holes and debris of battle and beside me were the remains of a Bosche who shuffled off this mortal coil in October and left it ill concealed, stuck out the side of the trench.'

In June 1918 in the Champagne 2nd and 3rd US Divisions were committed alongside the French to help stem the enemy offensive subsequently known as the Third Battle of the Aisne, when Ludendorff punched a 36-mile (58km) deep salient into the Allied lines. With the enemy now within 20 miles (32km) of their greatest advance in 1914, US Marines fought a sometimes confused pitched battle at Belleau Wood. Amos Wilder was with their supporting artillery:

'Yesterday went to the observation post on horseback with Lt Davis and Cpl Glorvigen. Rode a couple of kilometres along a road from which we could see the disputed country for miles through the intervals between clumps of trees. Marines in woods—food camouflaged—sleeping in little dug out places big enough for one. We go up a tree with

Opposite, below: *Doughboys bringing in German prisoners, watched by French troops. In the last weeks of the war German morale suffered in response to the defeats of the 'hundred days'. Despite some significant 'last stands', large numbers of prisoners were also taken during the retreat.*

Below: *The octagonal hunting lodge at Belleau Wood, scene of fighting involving US 2nd Division, June 1918. The Germans made an advance north of Chateau-Thierry, and 2nd Division, which included two regiments of US Marines, was moved up to support the French. From 6 June there were repeated and bloody attacks and counterattacks until the ground was secured by the Marines almost three weeks later. The shell-scarred lodge itself was a German HQ until taken by 43rd Company, USMC. The wood was quickly renamed the Bois de la Brigade de Marine: the commemorative plaque designed by Felix de Waldon was unveiled in 1955 by Gen L.C. Shepherd, who had himself served with the American Expeditionary Force.*

Photo By CHILJIAN

HUNTING LODGE BELLEAU WOODS

Above: *German troops 'louse hunting' in a bunker in the Argonne, 1917. Rats were obvious irritations, but lice tormented almost everyone not able to take baths or clean clothing. Often running seams of clothing across a candle and picking out eggs was the only method of relief.*

Below: *This photograph, by W. L. King, of Millersberg, Ohio, shows what the battlefields of the Western Front looked like in 1919. Suddenly the American public would become sickeningly familiar with hitherto obscure parts of rural France.*

glasses… targeting on a farmhouse. A Marine tells about classmates killed with half a battalion the night before. Some platoons still out there in those woods without communication, maybe prisoners—don't know where they are. More German shells in afternoon and during a barrage at night… Every A.M. for the last four or five days there has been a heavy barrage at dawn, following steady firing all night. We are directly opposite the Bois de Belleau which I think taken yesterday by Marines.'

With the opening of the Second Battle of the Marne on 15 July 1918, two German armies now squared up against Fifth and Sixth French armies. Alongside the 23 French divisions, and three furnished by the British and Italians, elements of nine US divisions were engaged. Marshal Foch launched his major counterstroke on 18 July, supported by over 2,000 guns, many of which were heavies, firing a rapid preparation, plus 350 tanks. As Foch observed the results obtained were 'considerable', and, 'apart from the ground gained, our advanced guards had reached the line Pernant–Neuilly Saint Front–Torcy, and Sixth and Tenth Armies had captured 10,000 prisoners and several hundred guns'. Foch thought a victory won, but by 20 July however enemy resistance had hardened considerably. Fighting would continue until 6 August. As Lt Walser wrote home to his family:

Right: *Sgt Alvin York won the Medal of Honor (presented to him by Black Jack Pershing) during the Meuse-Argonne offensive for leading an attack that took 32 machine guns, killed 28 German soldiers and captured 132 others—as so well portrayed by Gary Cooper.*

Below: *Congestion at the front. Lack of decent roads in the Argonne led to enormous traffic jams which held back the attack.*

Bottom: *The Meuse-Argonne American Cemetery and Memorial in France, covers 130.5 acres. Over 14,000—the largest number of US military dead in Europe—are buried here, most losing their lives during the Meuse-Argonne Offensive.*

'The American infantry has proved itself unquestionably to be the best in the world—a little too brave perhaps. Every one of them ought to have a DSO… The dead and wounded are harrowing sights, sometimes. Worst of all are the shell-shocked cases. Then as you go through a field you find a squad of Americans, lying as they fell, with faces and bayonets facing towards the enemy.'

If the Doughboy came of age, and of experience, in the Marne and Champagne, the same was not yet true of the high command. For Pershing had long since harboured both the ambition, and the mandate, to command US forces independently, on their own battlefront, in the victorious prosecution of the war. This would finally be answered when Allied partners agreed that the US Army would be used in the crushing of the St Mihiel salient. Two US Corps, the IV and I, would fight alongside each other, pushing broadly northward, smaller numbers of French would take the other side, advancing mainly West to East. As what was described as the first 'all-American' operation the proceedings of 12-13 September were closely observed. Despite heavy rain objectives were achieved, and honour satisfied. More Germans escaped from St Mihiel than had been hoped, but this was at least in part because they had apprehended that the salient was in danger, and prepared to withdraw.

The action at St Mihiel was terminated somewhat abruptly, but essentially because, with Allied efforts making good progress elsewhere, the US Army was required by Marshal Foch to take its place toward the right-hand end of what was now a vast advancing Allied line stretching all the way from Verdun to Ypres. The front now adopted by First US Army, three corps aligned abreast, was the Meuse-Argonne, stretching from the banks of the Meuse River in the east across to the depths of the Argonne forest in the west. Whilst parts of the new American sector were more hospitable, the rocky woodland of the Argonne was hardly an enticing place to fight. Nor was a massive redeployment at night an easy way to start a campaign. Three large divisions would head up each corps sector as the army rolled forward in battle. The divisions would put forward one brigade at a time and as each brigade became exhausted, it was planned to replace it with another. The battle commenced on 26 September. A total of 2,775 guns fired in support, half of these crewed by French troops, and 189 French tanks worked with

Below: *Wrecked trench in the aftermath of battle in the Argonne. Its walls are of both sandbags and wicker gabions.*

Bottom: *A French gas warning post during bad weather in the Champagne, c.1917. A sentry stands amidst a heap of sandbags, just peeping over the parapet. The alarm horn appears top left.*

Sommepy

Left: *The Sommepy American Monument on the Blanc Mont Ridge. Dedicated in 1937, this golden yellow tower of limestone with a viewing platform overlooking the battlefields commemorates the 70,000 Americans who served in this region during 1918. In the parkland around its base are the remains of trenches and gun emplacements. As the dedication here remarks:*

'In early July 1918 the 42nd American Division entered the battle lines with the 13th and 170th French divisions near Souain. There it gallantly assisted in repelling the last German major offensive of the war. When the allies began their great convergent offensive in late September, the 2nd and 36th American divisions were assigned to the French fourth army. On October 3 the 2nd division, supported on the left by the 167th, in a brilliant operation captured Blanc Mont Ridge on which this monument stands. The 36th division relieved the 2nd on October 10 and continued the advance northward as far as the Aisne River. Three infantry regiments of the 93rd American division, serving with the 157th and 161st French divisions, engaged in intermittent fighting during September and October taking part in the capture of Ripont, Sechault and Trieres Farm.'

Below: *A fire trench viewed from the Sommepy monument showing clearly the 'traverses' or shoulders that localised blast and prevented an attacking enemy from firing down the length of the trench. The monument occupies what was formerly a German vantage point.*

Right: *A US field wagon and a French 105mm gun at Fleury, Verdun. The wagon caption states that it was used for road maintenance during the Meuse-Argonne offensive of September–November 1918.*

Below: *A postcard sent by a soldier of Wurttemberg Infanterie Regiment Nr 127 showing a pen sketch of 'a captured English machine gun in the Argonne'. Vickers guns were also issued to early US forces in France. This weapon is emplaced behind sandbags and loophole plates, with a deeper excavation behind for the crew, one of whom stands sentry smoking his pipe in apparent unconcern.*

Eroberles engl. Masch. Gewehr in den Argonnen

the infantry, though a majority of the vehicles had US crews.

The Germans now faced unfavourable odds all along the line, and their first positions were taken quite rapidly. Nevertheless if anyone had expected operations to be easy, or cheap, they would quickly be disabused. Montfaucon was taken in bloody fighting on the second day, but fresh troops, under pressure to make rapid progress, were frequently caught by frontal or flanking fire from German machine guns when advancing into patches of open terrain. Another issue was that whilst the enemy were moving back the Americans had to advance guns and supplies across ground already ravaged by war. The tanks, though useful, did not have thick armour, and many suffered mechanical failures. The advance stopped on 28 September and deteriorated into attack and counterattack. Only six days later was forward movement resumed against the positions of the Kriemhilde Stellung, with the enemy defending the Romagne and Cunel heights, and Grandpre along the River Aire.

VARENNES-EN-ARGONNE - Monument commémoratif de l'Etat de Pensylvanie — State of Pensylvania Memorial

Right: *An interwar image of the impressive Pennsylvania State Memorial erected in 1927 at Varrenes en Argonne.*

Opposite: *A French Canon de 155mm GPF, 1917, on display at Fort Pompelle. This powerful piece was one of the first to use a split-trailed carriage, and was capable of blasting a 95lb (43kg) shell over 10 miles (16km). The weapon was used by both French and American forces.*

Edit. Magasins Réunis

Meuse-Argonne Cemetery
Right: *The central pool of the Meuse-Argonne cemetery. Comprising 130 acres, with 14,246 graves, this cemetery contains the largest number of American dead in any US European military burial ground. More than another 900 are commemorated on 'Tablets of the Missing'.*

Left: *Most of the dead at the Meuse-Argonne fell in the offensive of the same name, the graves being laid out with geometric precision in eight large plots. There would be even more, were it not for the fact that, unlike several other nations, the US allowed its citizens to repatriate the bodies of their fallen relatives home from the battlefields. This is just one row of the 486 of the dead at the Meuse-Argonne Cemetery who are, in the words of the memorials, 'known but to God'. Also interred at the cemetery are several Medal of Honor winners. These include 'balloon buster' flying ace Lt Frank Luke, Lt Erwin R. Bleckley, Capt Marcellus H. Chiles, Cpl Harold W. Roberts, Sgt William Sawelson, Maj Oscar F. Miller and Lt-Col Fred E. Smith. African-American Cpl Freddie Stowers was left leading a platoon during the attack on Hill 188 in September 1918 and died in the advance, but waited 73 years for the posthumous award of his medal. Sgt Matej Kocak, USMC, was awarded both the Army and Navy Medal of Honor.*

Below left: *The grave of Maj Oscar F. Miller, Medal of Honor, died September 1918, Meuse-Argonne cemetery. As his medal citation relates:*

'After two days of intense physical and mental strain, during which Major Miller had led his battalion in the front line of the advance through the forest of Argonne, the enemy was met in a prepared position south of Gesnes. Though almost exhausted, he energetically reorganized his battalion and ordered an attack. Upon reaching open ground the advancing line began to waver in the face of machinegun fire from the front and flanks and direct artillery fire. Personally leading his command group forward between his front-line companies, Major Miller inspired his men by his personal courage, and they again pressed on toward the hostile position. As this officer led the renewed attack he was shot in the right leg, but he nevertheless staggered forward at the head of his command. Soon afterwards he was again shot in the right arm, but he continued the charge, personally cheering his troops on through the heavy machinegun fire. Just before the objective was reached he received a wound in the abdomen, which forced him to the ground, but he continued to urge his men on, telling them to push on to the next ridge and leave him where he lay. He died from his wounds a few days later.'

Navarin Farm

The ossuary monument to the dead of the armies of the Champagne occupies the site of the old Navarin Farm at the epicentre of the battlefield. The foundation stone of the pyramid, which originated from the ruined church at Souain, was laid in 1923 in the presence of US ambassador Myron Herrick. The monument was dedicated the following year by Marshal Joffre. The monument contains a chapel and a crypt in which is interred the remains of 10,000 men. The various divisions involved on this sector are listed on the front of the monument (**Below right**).

Right: *A view across an undisturbed piece of battlefield to the Navarin Farm monument. This picture was taken from a shell hole, and the visitors on the left are standing atop a small mound serving as viewing point. Fighting in the vicinity continued from 1915 to 1918, ultimately involving 107 French and Allied divisions. These included four of the US Army, the 2nd, 36th, 42nd and the African-American 93rd. This last included regiments such as the 369th 'Harlem Hellfighters' and the 370th 'Black Devils'.*

Left: *Detail of the three figues on the Navarin Farm ossuary created by Maxime Real del Sarte (1888–1954). Sarte was himself a war veteran, wounded at Éparges in 1916, where he lost his lower left arm. No longer able to wield hammer and chisel, he produced designs and models, subsequently realised in stone by his assistants. The figures here are an American soldier, modelled on Quentin Roosevelt, a nephew of the US President killed in air combat in 1918; a French grenadier with the features of Gen Gouraud (1867–1946); and, foreground, a French soldier based on the artist's brother killed on the Chemin des Dames. Gen Gouraud, who commanded at—and was wounded in—the Dardanelles campaign, led the French Fourth Army in 1916 to 1918. After the war he held various colonial positions and helped raise the funds for the monument. He was himself interred here.*

Montfaucon American Monument
Inaugurated in 1937, Montfaucon is located 7 miles (14km) south of the Meuse-Argonne Cemetery and commemorates the campaign of 26 September to 11 November 1918. It is topped with a statue of liberty, and the walls of the foyer show an engraved map of the operations.

Right: *There are 234 steps inside the massive Doric column of the Montfaucon American Monument. At the top is an observation platform overlooking the battlefields.*

Below: *The ruins of the abbey church at Montfaucon, quite literally in the shadow of the American Monument. Along with nearby bunkers, the church formed part of the German defences. The oblong block, left, camouflaged to appear part of the ruined church, is in fact an observation post.*

Chateau-Thierry American Monument

Visitors' vehicles are dwarfed by the monument, designed by Paul Philippe Cret. Located on Hill 204 the monument marks the opening of the offensive of 18 July 1918, and its platform provides broad views over the Marne valley. The massive figures sculpted by Alfred Bottiau represent France, right, and America, left.

CHAPTER 8

THE LAST YEAR:
CAMBRAI AND THE
GREEN FIELDS BEYOND

The German burial ground at Clausen, Luxembourg City, containing 196 burials from 1914–18. The position of Luxembourg was ambiguous: the tiny army of the Grand Duchy did not resist German entry in 1914, but a protest was issued, and some of her citizens fled to joint the Entente. There was apprehension that Luxembourg would now be annexed, but with Allied victory and the Armistice, German forces were ejected and US troops marched in.

Opposite: *The colourful French village memorial at Ayette. Scene of heavy fighting involving British 31st and 32nd Divisions in March and April 1918, the village also boasts an unusual Chinese and Indian cemetery. Nearby Bucquoy, roughly equidistant between Albert and Arras, was where Whippet tanks made their debut.*

Below: *The battle of Cambrai is commemorated by the Royal Tank Regiment as a significant milestone in the development of the tank. In fact, the use of tanks was inflated postwar by armour proponents Fuller and Lidell Hart. The battle was a game of two halves: the first attack saw the British achieve complete surprise and make significant inroads into the German lines; however, the German counterattack nullified those gains and restored the status quo. However, the British had shown that the Hindenburg Line could be pierced.*

By late 1917 the Western Front had ossified for three years. Nevertheless, this was not a war fought in isolation, and there had been some movement, including the German retreat to the Hindenburg Line.

Technology and tactics had advanced both in the air and on land, and attrition combined with successes and failures on the Eastern Front, plus the entry of new combatants tipped advantage, first one way then the other. British and French tanks, used in growing numbers, were one imponderable. For whilst the Germans did not produce any of their own until 1918, this was still one Allied superiority yet to show its full potential. Though the attack at Cambrai did not result in a war-winning breakthough, tanks combined with more imaginative use of artillery, and the enemy response which regained much of the ground taken, were signs that the tyranny of solid fronts might one day be broken.

The British plan aimed at Cambrai because it was a key node in the Hindenburg Line, and the nearby Bourlon Ridge could threaten to unhinge the German position to the north. As Capt Geoffrey Dugdale recalled:

'Each battalion was to attack with 18 tanks, and the tanks were to attack in groups of three to form a triangle. There were six groups of tanks attacking in a line with each battalion. There were supply tanks, tanks especially equipped with wire-cutting apparatus, and several which had a roving commission, i.e. the commander had orders to keep his eyes open, and to chip in if he saw any of our troops in difficulties. There were 407 tanks employed in this battle. This was the first time in the war that we had ever attempted a large surprise attack against a very powerful line of trenches such as the Hindenburg Line. In front of us there were no less than three rows of intact wire. None of our artillery had been registered before the battle, and the gunners could therefore only fire by the map. It was arranged that all the wire cutting

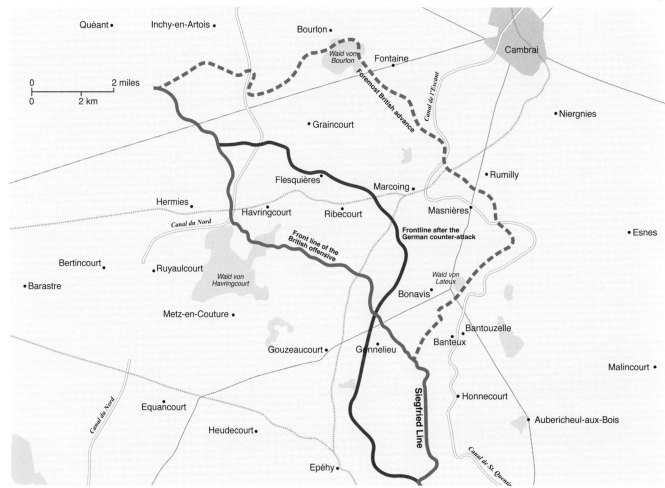

and flattening should be done by the tanks, and that the infantry should follow behind them through the wire.'

Tanks were also employed in various support roles, and many were equipped with a 'fascine' of brushwood on their top deck. This could be dropped into enemy trenches so creating an instant, if temporary, bridge.

The attack, which began on the morning of 20 November to the sound of a thousand guns, started well. Smoke and a creeping barrage helped the tanks and six infantry divisions forward, and it was hoped that cavalry could now be able to exploit a promising situation. West of Flesquières 62nd Division reached the edge of the woods on the Bourlon Ridge, and though 180 tanks were out of commission by the end of the day of these only 65 were knocked out due to enemy action, and many could later be made serviceable. Yet driving, even surviving, inside one of these slow-moving monsters was an experience never forgotten, as an officer commanding a section of H Battalion at Cambrai explained of his experience on as the attack continued the next day:

'All I could see through a revolver loophole was *Hong Kong* [H Battalion machines had names beginning with that letter] slightly ahead and about 200 yards to our left. She was coming in for the fury of the guns... Now it was our turn. Shells were bursting all around us and fragments of them were striking the sides of the tank. Each of our six-pounders required a gun layer and a gun loader, and while these four men blazed away, the rest of the perspiring crew kept the tank zig-zagging to upset the enemy's aim. It was a hard job to turn one of these early tanks. It needed four of the crew to work the levers, and they took their orders by signals. First of all the tank had to stop. A knock on the right side would attract the attention of the right gearsman. The driver would hold a clenched fist, which was the signal to put the track into neutral. The gearsman would repeat the signal to show it was done. The officer, who controlled the break levers, would pull the right one, which held the right track. The driver would accelerate and the tank would slew round slowly on the stationary right track while the left track went

Opposite, above: *German troops advance through the Somme village of Etricourt, 1918. The Germans came this way in March, and by popular account the village had been 'totally destroyed' by November.*

Opposite, below: *Etricourt as it appears today. Much may have been lost or damaged but the layout of this road is recognisably similar to a century ago.*

Below left: *Machine gun-armed British female Mk IV Chaperon II of 9th Company, C Battalion, Tank Corps, commanded by 2-Lt Annett, was knocked out by enemy artillery near Lateau Wood, during the battle of Cambrai, November 1917. The Ace of Spades was the sign of 12th Eastern Division who worked in concert with tanks during the operation. One tank bearing Ace of Spades markings was captured by the Germans and renamed Schnuki (later Kerlchen). In 1918 it served with Oberleutnant Wilhelm's Nr 13 detachment of captured armour.*

Below: *German postcard showing a tattered French NCO captured in the Argonne.*

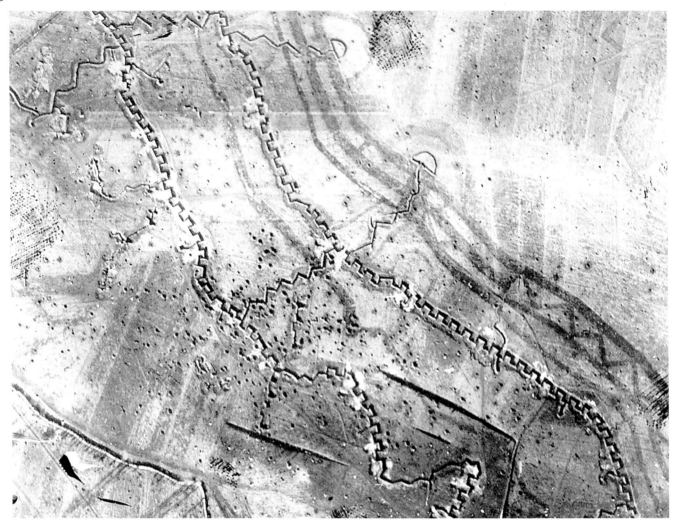

Above: *Front-line trenches near Cambrai, seen from the air. The shadowy lines are belts of barbed wire, on the front edge of which can be seen advanced listening posts. The crenellated lines are fire trenches with their distinctive fire bays and traverses. Zigzagging communication trenches allow troops and supplies to move in and out of the front lines. The pockmarks are shell holes.*

Opposite: *French memorial at Gouzeaucourt. The village was retaken in early 1917, but fell during the Cambrai counterattack on 30 November. The same evening it was wrested back by 1st Battalion, Irish Guards. Lost for a third time on 22 March 1918, it was recaptured towards the end of the war. It was also the place where, in 1917, the first Americans serving with a US Army unit were wounded in the front line. The village is mentioned in Rudyard Kipling's 'The Irish Guards', and is the title of a poem by Edmund Blunden.*

into motion. As soon as the tank had turned sufficiently the procedure was reversed. Zig-zagging was, therefore, a slow and complicated business. In between pulls on his brakes the tank commander fired the front machine gun. Our only hope of salvation was to keep going and follow as erratic a course as possible. Just at this critical moment the Autovac, supplying petrol to the engine, failed. The engine spluttered and stopped.'

Nevertheless casualty rates, though substantial, were markedly lower than at Passchendaele. Yet, as resistance stiffened the pace slowed in subsequent days, with fierce German counterattacks beginning as reinforcements were rushed to stem the rupture. By 28 November the advance had reached high tide. The British now attempted to consolidate a salient approximately six miles by seven (10 by 11km) with its front along the ridge. Thereafter, the enemy recovered his composure, beginning his own counter-offensive on 30 November. Again the early phase of the German attack was quite successful. Just one in the vanguard was Vizefeldwebel Engesser of *Fusilier Regiment Nr 40*:

'In no time at all we were in possession of the first enemy positions. Without pausing we assaulted the next hollow, where we came across numerous dugouts. We had soon cleared the enemy out of them. Up to this point, about 200m (650ft), we had doubled forward. I commanded the light machine guns, whose crews found the advance exceptionally strenuous because of their heavy loads. Despite the great effort involved, we stormed forward onto the hill to our front and, once again, we soon broke through the tough defence of the enemy. We took numerous

Opposite, above right: *A cheery German soldier at a gas alarm post, complete with bell. The soldier carries his own mask in the tin cylinder.*

Opposite, above left: *Pte Ellison, the last British soldier to die, lies within a few feet of the first, the young Pte Parr, at St Symphorien. George Edwin Ellison of Leeds, a former regular soldier, had also been a coal miner. When he died on 11 November 1918 he was a 40-year old father of two and serving with the 5th (Royal Irish) Lancers.*

Opposite, below: *Map showing the last year of the war—first, the German gains during the Spring Offensive; then the Allied response that led to the Armistice.*

Below: *Men of the East Lancashire Regiment in a sap head near Givenchy. Notice the use of a camouflaged trench periscope.*

prisoners. We continued on unstoppably through the next dip, clearing the dugouts by use of hand grenades and were on our way to assaulting the next hill when we came under heavy small-arms fire. Our ranks had already been thinned…'

The German fight back was a bitter disappointment. As the British Official History remarked, bringing home to many soldiers 'that the German Army was by no means as "dead" as some people fondly imagined.' Though the picture of Cambrai as epoch-making 'tank battle' may have been over-drawn, it did point the way to a different future. This was one in which not only tanks were more important, but new infantry tactics developed through the fire of war came to the fore, and artillery barrages, lasting hours rather than days, were directed very specifically to support those infantry.

Sadly for the Allied cause the battles of attrition waged at such cost in 1916 and 1917 had not achieved their objective. Indeed, far from producing a balance of power favourable to the Allies, 1918 dawned with a modest German preponderance of strength on the Western Front. Curiously this came about less due to French and British casualties, but more because Russia had finally collapsed. Food shortages and strikes early in 1917 were followed by the abdication of the Tsar in the wake of the February Revolution. A provisional committee was appointed but the Kerensky summer offensive failed. In October came the Bolshevik Revolution, and the Winter Palace was stormed. Lenin returned to Russia, receiving assisted passage through German territory, and a Decree on Peace was promptly issued. Though the Treaty of Brest Litovsk was not concluded until the following March Russia was out of the war, and over winter much of the German Army in the east was transferred to the west. At the end of October 1917 the Allies had 176 infantry divisions on the Western Front against 150 German. By New Year's Eve the balance was almost even, with 168 Allied facing 171 German. As of mid-March 1918 there were 169 Allied, but 192 German. As yet US forces on the Western Front were still negligible, little more than six divisions, representing barely 5 percent of the Allied strength. For a brief window of opportunity Germany had the advantage, it was a choice of attacking or remaining passive as Allied forces expanded and by 1919 would achieve overwhelming strength.

So it was that on 21 March 1918 Germany launched what was billed as the 'Peace Offensive', or 'Kaiser's Battle', intended to finish the war once and for all. The attackers were concealed by fog, as was reported by Bavarian Leutnant Reinhold Spengler:

'We were surrounded by acrid cordite smoke and dense fog and could see only a few metres. The main orientation was only possible by the whizzing of our shells and the noticeable direction of the fire. Watch in hand, I was able at first to follow the creeping barrage with my light machine gun section but, because of the increasing noise of battle, it became more difficult to rely on the right direction by ear. After about 2,000ft (600m), tall, thin soldiers with broad brimmed, flat steel helmets emerged from the

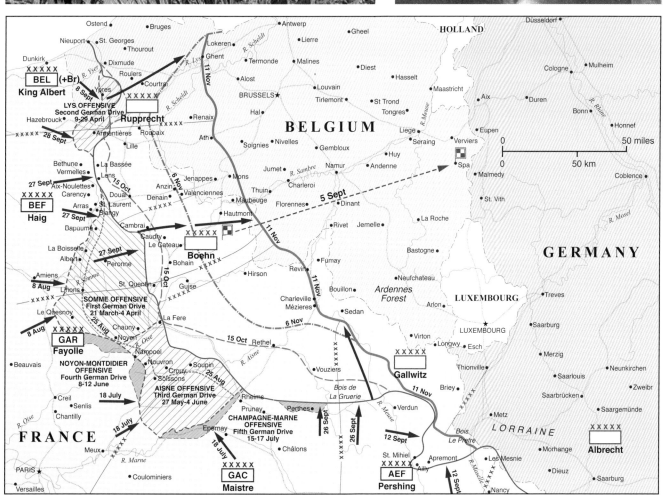

Above right: *British troops after battle. Foreground is a Lewis .303-inch light machine gun and a box of Mills bombs. Both weapons were introduced to the British infantry during the war adding considerably to their battlefield repertoire.*

Dormans Memorial Chapel Opposite: *The town of Dormans was almost totally destroyed during the two battles of the Marne, and Marshal Foch chose this site, with panoramic views, to commemorate the action. Steps connect a sombre crypt below to a chapel above, and to a balcony atop the monument.*

Above left: *View from the Dormans chapel over the cloister and ossuary. The remains of 1,500 men, Allied and German, are interred in the crypt, which also contains other relics including a death mask of Marshal Ferdinand Foch (1851–1929) Allied Commander-in-Chief from 1918.*

fog. We didn't know who they were, having always had the French as opponents before. These men were all pitiful young Englishmen. They had no weapons and their raised arms indicated their surrender. Coming closer, one could see their faces were marked by the terrible events of the last hours.'

Within three weeks the advance had swallowed 40 miles (65km), a figure only dreamed of since 1914. Thereafter, one offensive was followed by another, on the Chemin des Dames, towards Paris, and finally on the Marne in July: but with each successive thrust, gains were smaller and smaller. Hindenburg and Ludendorff were exhausting the German armies more quickly than the Allies were giving way. Dangerously as the Spring Offensive had begun, it would prove a sort of pyrrhic victory.

On 8 August came what was arguably the turning point, the Black Day of the German Army, on which major Allied offensives were launched between the Ancre and the Avre, soon extending to the Oise. So began the 'Hundred Days' leading to the end of the war. By the end of September the Germans were back to St Quentin. At first the retreat was highly orderly and repeated stands were supported by artillery and machine guns causing heavy casualties to the troops fighting them back. By October however a new grand offensive was propelling the Germans across Belgium, who were also forced to give up much of the occupied area of France. The Hindenburg Line was breached, and the British were across the River Lys.

The events of 1918 are instructive, both tactically and historically. However it is worth bearing in mind that, compared with earlier static campaigns on the Western Front, with their laboriously constructed forts and defences, the 1918 war of movement left far fewer long term impressions on the landscape. To this extent they are a warning that an attempt to 'read' the battlefields based on physical and archaeological observation alone is fraught with danger, for only by using the Western Front together with all other types of evidence can we hope to understand the war that so obviously failed 'to end all wars'.

The Arrival of the Tank

Right: *An interwar photo of a much shot about and corroded British Mk IV tank displayed at Ypres station. The Mk IV, introduced in 1917, was the commonest British tank of the war. Weighing 28 tons it could manage a steady 4mph (7kph) and had a maximum armour thickness of about half an inch (12.5mm). Though better protected than the Mk I it was still vulnerable to artillery fire.*

Below right: *A model Whippet tank on the Flers memorial. First produced in 1917 the British Whippet was intended to be a faster, cheaper tank than the familiar slow rhomboid forms that first saw action the previous year. The crew was only three, and the armament four machine guns. Weighing 14 tons the Whippet could manage 8mph (13kph), not very fast but considerably faster than its predecessors.*

Bottom right: *German A7V tanks. Designed and built under the direction of Joseph Vollmer, the A7V was the first German tank, and though trials took place in 1917 it did not see combat until March 1918. The first tank versus tank action was against the British the following month at Villers-Bretonneux. The A7V was something of a monster with six machine guns, a 57mm gun, and a crew of 18. Its off road performance was modest and very few were produced.*

Opposite: *New technology in the museum at Meaux. Underneath the French fighter are (right) a 105mm gun and (left) a Renault light tank. The Renault FT17 was an advanced design, being the first to have a fully rotating turret. Over 3,000 were manufactured, most in 1918. The so-called 'Six-Ton Tank' was also used by the US Army.*

Somme American cemetery
*The Somme American cemetery and memorial at Bony, Picardy, 13 miles north of St Quentin, commemorates those who served in US units attached to British armies or in operations near Cantigny. The 14 acres (5.6ha) of grounds contain the remains of 1,844 military dead, and a further 333 of the missing are recorded on the walls. The architect for the memorial chapel was George Howe of Philadelphia. The cemetery contains the bodies of many who fought at Cambrai, Hamel, in front of Amiens and in other actions from the latter part of the war. The 1st, 27th, 30th, 33rd and 80th US Infantry divisions are all represented. First opened as a temporary cemetery in 1918, Bony was later used to concentrate the graves from other burial grounds in the area. The base of the flagpole is decorated with cast bronze representations of American helmets (**Opposite**). One of the dead here, 1-Lt William T. Fitzsimons (1889–1917) was the first US officer to be killed in action. Fitzsimons was serving as a doctor with US Army Base Hospital #5, near Dannes-Camiers in the Pas de Calais, when he and three private soldiers were killed in an air raid.*

Above: *British and French POWs being marched along a road near Reims, summer 1918. At the head of the column two British officers hide their faces from the camera. The German army continued to attack until July, lapping around both flanks of Reims, reaching their furthest point of advance around 15 July. The tide finally turned three days later with French counterattacks, and Gen von Boehn's Seventh Army, which had crossed the Marne, was withdrawn.*

Right: *Mossy and battered German bunker at Montfaucon. The hilltop village with its important observation point had been occupied for four years and was reinforced by four successive lines of defence by the time it was assaulted by the US Army in September 1918. Several such bunkers are scattered in the grounds around the ruins and monument.*

BIBLIOGRAPHY

Anon: *Battlefields of the Marne, 1914*; Michelin, London, 1919.

Anon: *Das Fort Douaumont und Seine Rolle in der Schlacht von Verdun*; Fremont, Verdun, 1931.

Anon: *Trench Fortifications of the Western Front*; Imperial War Museum, London, 1998.

Alstein, Maarten van: *The Great War Remembered*; Flemish Peace Institute, Brussels, 2011.

Audoine-Rouuzeau, Stephane & Becker: *1914–1918: Understanding the Great War*; Profile, London, 2002.

Barton, Peter (et al): *Beneath Flanders Fields*; Spellmount, Staplehurst, 2004.

Blond, Georges: *The Marne* (English Trans); Prion, London, 2002.

Brown, Malcolm: *The Imperial War Museum Book of the Western Front*; Sidgwick & Jackson, London, 1993.

_____: *Verdun, 1916*; Tempus, Stroud, 1999.

Buchner, Adolf: *Der Minenkrieg auf Vauquois*; Deutenhausen, 1982.

Bull, Stephen: *An Officer's Manual of the Western Front, 1914–1918*; Conway, London, 2008.

Cave, Nigel: *Arras: Vimy Ridge*; Pen and Sword, Barnsley, 1996.

Chasseaud, Peter; *Topography of Armageddon*; Mapbooks, Lewes, 1991.

Clayton, Anne: *Chevasse Double VC*; Leo Cooper, London, 1992.

Clayton, P.B.: *Tales of Talbot House 1915–1918*, new edition; Toc H, London, 1945.

Coombes, Rose E.B.: *Before Endeavours Fade*; After the Battle, London, 1983.

Corrigan, Gordon: *Mud, Blood and Poppycock*; Cassell, London, 2003.

Desfosses, Yves (et al): *L'Archeologie de la Grande Guerre*; Ouest-France, Rennes, 2008.

Dunn, J.C.: *The War the Infantry Knew*; Cardinal, London, 1987.

Edmonds J.E. (et al): *History of the Great War Based on Official Documents*; HMSO, London, (29 volumes) 1923–1946.

Ellis, John: *Eye-Deep in Hell*; Croom Helm, London, 1976.

Gebsattel, Ludwig von: *Von Nancy bis zum Camp des Romains, 1914*; Stalling, Berlin, 1928.

Gliddon, Gerald: *The Battle of the Somme: A Topographical History*; Sutton, Stroud, 1994.

Hardt, Fred B.: *Die Deutschen Schuetzengraben und Soldatenzeitungen*; R. Piper, Munich, 1917.

Men of German 38th Division man a front-line trench in a wooded area near Tracy le Val, south of the Oise, April 1916. Trunks have been used to create a fire step, and branches trimmed to revet the trench. This was a comparative quiet sector but in May the division was shifted to Verdun where they lost about half their numbers in the battles around Hill 304.

Hart, Peter: *The Somme*; Weidenfeld and Nicholson, London, 2005.

Henniker, A.M.: *Transportation on the Western Front*; HMSO, London, 1937.

Holmes, Richard: *The Western Front*; London, 1999.

_____: Tommy: *The British Soldier on the Western Front 1914–1918*; Harper Collins, London, 2004.

Holt, Tonie & Valmai: *Battlefields of the First World War*; Pavilion, London, 1995.

Kearsey A.: *1915 Campaign In France: The Battles of Aubers Ridge, Festubert and Loos*; reprinted Eastbourne, 2002.

Joffre, Joseph J.C. (et al): *The Two Battles of the Marne*; Thornton Butterworth, London, 1927.

Longworth, Philip: *The Unending Vigil: A History of the Commonwealth War Graves Commission*; Constable, London, 1967.

Masefield, John: *The Old Front Line*; originally published 1917, new edn with an introduction by Howard Green, Spurbooks, Bourne End, 1972.

Oldham, Peter: *Pill Boxes of the Western Front*; Leo Cooper, London, 1995.

Orain, Philippe (ed): *Les Champs de Bataille: Verdun, Argonne, Saint-Mihiel*; Michelin, Boulogne-Billancourt, 2011.

Pelletier-Wilkins, Rosalind: *The Forgotten Front : Artois 1914–1918*; Tilloy-lès-Mofflaines, 2007.

Rawling, Bill: Surviving Trench Warfare: *Technology and the Canadian Corps 1914-1918*; University of Toronto Press, 1992.

Richter, Oliver: *Grabenkrieg*; two vols, Vollert, Erlangen, 2012.

Robbins, Keith: *The First World War*; Oxford University Press, 1984.

Saunders, Nicholas J.: Killing Time: *Archaeology and the First World War*; Sutton, Stroud, 2007.

Stedman, Michael: *Guillemont*; Pen and Sword, Barnsley, 1998.

Stosch, Albrecht von: *Somme-Nord II Teil: Die Brennpunkte der Schlacht*; Stalling, Berlin, 1927.

Ulrich, Bernd (et al): *German Soldiers in the Great War: Letters and Eyewitness Accounts*; Pen & Sword, Barnsley, 2010.

Vogel, Stosch (et al): *Schlachten des Weltkrieges*; Reichsarchiv, Berlin, (38 volumes) 1921–1930.

Willman, Georg: *Kriegsgraeber in Europa*; Bertelsmann, Munich, 1980.

Winter, Jay: *Sites of Memory, Sites of Mourning: The Great War in European Cultural History*; Cambridge University Press, 1995.

Wirth, A.: *Der Kampf um den Hartmannsweilerkopf 1914–1918*; Brand, 1988.

French postwar Verdun poster, produced by the French railway company Chemins de Fer de l'Est.

INDEX